WORLD AGRICULTURAL DEVELOPMENT AND THE FUTURE OF U.S. AGRICULTURE

A WORLD AGRICULTURAL DEVELOPMENT AND THE FUTURE OF U.S. AGRICULTURE

BY JOHN M. ANTLE

WITHDRAWN

American Enterprise Institute for Public Policy Research

Washington, D.C.

Distributed by arrangement with

UPA, Inc.
4720 Boston Way
Lanham, Md. 20706
3 Henrietta Street
London WC2E 8LU England

Library of Congress Cataloging-in-Publication Data

Antle, John M.
    World agricultural development and the future of U.S. agriculture
    John M. Antle.
        p.   cm. — (AEI studies ; 470)
    ISBN 0-8447-3651-1 (alk. paper)
        1. Agriculture—Economic aspects—United States—Forecasting.
    2. Produce trade—United States—Forecasting.   3. Agriculture-
    -Economic aspects—Forecasting.   4. Produce trade—Forecasting.
    I. Title.   II. Series.
    HD1761.A75   1988
    338.1'0973—dc19   88-3351
                                                                          CIP

1   3   5   7   9   10   8   6   4   2

AEI Studies 470

Printed in the United States of America

About the Author

John M. Antle is an associate professor in the Department of Agricultural Economics and Economics at Montana State University. He received his Ph.D. in economics from the University of Chicago in 1980. Since then he has been an assistant and associate professor at the University of California, Davis, a visiting professor at the University of Maryland, and a visiting fellow at Resources for the Future, in Washington, D.C. He has served as an economic consultant to international agricultural research centers and has traveled extensively in North Africa and Asia. His published research spans the fields of agricultural production, agricultural development, applied econometrics, resource economics, and international trade.

Contents

LIST OF TABLES

LIST OF FIGURES

Preface

This study was initiated in the spring of 1985 when the 1985 farm bill was being hotly discussed in Washington, D.C. After the roller-coaster ride that U.S. agriculture had taken in the 1970s and 1980s, policy makers and economic prognosticators alike were wondering what the future of U.S. agriculture is likely to be in the context of the changes that have been taking place and are continuing to take place in agricultures around the world. Without this answer, it certainly becomes difficult to discuss policy reform for agriculture rationally, especially with a longer perspective in mind.

In this context I was asked to prepare a study examining the longer-run prospects for U.S. agriculture, with emphasis on the effects of changes in developing agricultures. I have to thank Tom Johnson and Bruce Gardner for having confidence in me to undertake this large question. I also have to thank them for their patience in waiting for a long overdue product from me.

During the researching and writing of this study, I was on leave from the University of California, Davis, during 1985 and the first half of 1986, at Resources for the Future and at the University of Maryland, and then back at Davis in 1986 and 1987 when it was completed. I wish to thank these organizations for their generous support, which contributed to the final product. At Davis I was lucky to have Ken Foster's research assistance. His tireless searching for and assembling of sources and data added much to the study.

1
Introduction and Summary

The waste and distress resulting from the agricultural depression have forcibly shown the need of a sound long-time policy for the development of our agriculture. The welfare of millions of our people must not again be placed in jeopardy.

We must develop a well-balanced agriculture which will give farmers a fair share in the national income. Farming must be made to yield a return which will enable the rural population to maintain standards of living that are consistent with American ideals. The era of cheap, virgin land is now past. In the future, farmers must receive their financial rewards, not in higher land values, but in annual profits from their productive efforts. Though surplus production now depresses prices, the day is not so very far distant when our population will consume all we now produce and then press for more. We shall then have the problem of providing larger food supplies at prices that will be reasonable to the consumer and that will at the same time give the producer a fair return for his capital and labor. And in building for the future we must not fail to keep a watchful eye on the conservation of our agricultural resources for the use of generations yet to come.

Production of farm products in excess of effective demand has been a recurring cause of low returns in farming. At various times in our national development the distorted relation between supply of farm products and the demand for them has resulted in depressing prices below profitable levels. While it is extremely difficult to maintain a nice balance between supply and demand in the case of agricultural products, yet it may be possible to reduce, if not prevent, the serious maladjustments which prove so harmful.[1]

This quotation from a 1925 book by Henry A. Wallace, secretary of agriculture under Franklin D. Roosevelt, summarizes the issues that have been central to U.S. agricultural policy during the twentieth century. It expresses the attitude toward farming that continues to prevail today: that agriculture is a chronically disadvantaged sector that must be given a fair share of national income. It also anticipates

1

concerns recently raised by rapid population growth and environmental degradation.

Considering the far-reaching technological and economic changes that U.S. agriculture has undergone in the past fifty years, it is remarkable that the concerns of Wallace in the 1920s remain the concerns of U.S. agriculture and agricultural policy. Wallace did not anticipate the potential for technological innovation in agriculture, nor did he see agricultural issues as international in their scope and significance. But we should not fault him on that score; even today we have only begun to understand the economic, social, and political effects of the technological revolution in agriculture, which began as recently as the 1950s. To understand the likely future of U.S. agriculture, we must appreciate that attitudes toward agriculture that prevailed fifty years ago still shape our conception of it and our policies toward it.

We must also appreciate the changes that have taken place both nationally and internationally. Although the moral and emotional basis for public concern about the future of agriculture is much the same today as in Wallace's time, the technological and economic realities are very different. The latter half of the twentieth century has seen technological innovation in agriculture—both biological and mechanical—on a scale unimaginable in Wallace's time. Agricultural production, marketing, and policy decisions are based not only on regional or national but on international considerations. Agriculture in the late 1980s and beyond must be understood in a global context.

This study uses economic principles to assess likely patterns of agricultural development in the coming decades in light of historical events, current trends, and projections of future trends in key variables. The goal is to provide the information needed to answer these kinds of questions:

- What have been the long-run trends in global or agricultural production, prices, and trade, and what are they likely to be in the coming decades?
- What role will technological change and population growth play in future U.S. and world agricultural development?
- Will U.S. agriculture flourish in an interdependent world economy, or will it decline because of growing foreign competition?
- Does U.S. technical assistance to developing countries help or harm U.S. agriculture?
- What role will agricultural policy play in the future of U.S. agriculture? Are present policies adequate to deal with agriculture's future problems? If not, how do they need to be changed?

This chapter provides an overview of the issues addressed in this study and a summary of its findings. Chapter 2 introduces basic concepts of agricultural development; chapter 3 offers a theoretical analysis of the principles governing agricultural growth and trade; chapters 4 and 5 review past trends and future projections of key economic data; and chapter 6 synthesizes the analyses and data of chapters 3, 4, and 5 and uses their conclusions to address the questions raised above.

Overview

The analysis of world agricultural development presented in this study leads to the proposition that global technological change and economic development in open economies cause a predictable global pattern of the use of agricultural resources. This pattern involves a relative and absolute decline in the use of resources, particularly human labor, in agriculture. A similar pattern of resource use and agricultural change has been observed within the closed agricultural economies of the nineteenth and early twentieth centuries. Because of the increasing openness of modern economies to international trade, however, this pattern need not prevail nationally. Some countries' production may expand while others' contracts, the results depending on their resource endowments, technologies, and policies.

Trade makes it possible for countries to gain by exporting goods that they produce relatively more efficiently in exchange for those that they produce relatively less efficiently. By thus exploiting their comparative advantage, countries endowed with favorable conditions for agriculture can make themselves better off by producing a surplus of agricultural commodities and trading them for other goods. That such gains from trade are possible is one of the most fundamental insights of economic theory.

The role of trade in a country's economic well-being must be understood in the context of real-world factors not accounted for in the theory of comparative advantage. Government price, trade, and general economic policies may distort prices so that production patterns do not agree with those implied by comparative advantage. In a world of technological change, comparative advantage is a dynamic phenomenon defined in part by investment in the various forms of capital needed for technological change in agriculture, including physical infrastructure, agricultural research, on-farm physical capital, the education of farm people, and institutional change. Non-economic factors, such as political instability, distort economic

3

incentives and discourage the capital investments needed for a country to exploit its comparative advantage.

Market distortions and government intervention can and in the short run do move individual countries' patterns of resource use away from those implied by comparative advantage. Nevertheless, in the aggregate and the longer run, the historical record shows that economic forces do tend to drive resource allocation toward the pattern predicted by economic theory.

Modern agricultural technology, combined with innovations in transport technology, has enabled the highly productive regions of the world to provide an abundance of food domestically and also to export large amounts. One of the most significant changes in world agriculture since the 1960s has been the movement of large quantities of cereals from food-surplus to food-deficit regions of the world. To a large degree this pattern of food trade reflects patterns of population growth.

In the 1970s pessimists raised the specter of global hunger as projections of exponential population growth swamped predicted growth in production. While these predictions have proved to be wrong and population growth rates now appear to be declining in many parts of the world, population is expected to increase from 4.5 to 6 billion by the year 2000. The prospect of continued population growth suggests that large movements of food will continue.

Numerous economic and political problems arise in facilitating the massive movements of food required to feed a rapidly growing world population. One way to attack the world food problem is through food aid from the food-surplus to the food-deficit countries. But there is little agreement on how desirable direct food aid is or how it should be financed. Among its undesirable consequences, for example, are depressed producers' prices in the recipient countries, which stifle domestic incentives to produce. Low agricultural prices imply lower incomes of already poor farmers and swell the migration of rural people to crowded urban areas.

As an alternative to direct food aid, the high-income countries have contributed to the poor countries' productive capacity through technical assistance. Such policies have seen both successes and failures, in part because of limited transferability of biological technology. The establishment of international research centers has contributed significantly to the development of crop varieties suitable to conditions in food-deficit regions of the world. But technical aid has become as controversial as food aid. Groups representing U.S. agricultural interests have recently argued that U.S. foreign agri-

4

cultural assistance has stimulated production in developing countries and increased the competition facing U.S. producers of traded agricultural commodities. Economists have argued, however, that technical assistance leads to income growth and thus stimulates demand in recipient countries for the exports of the donor country.

Since the United States is one of the largest agricultural producers and the largest agricultural exporter in the world, the future of U.S. agriculture will be closely linked to the future of world agricultural development. But will U.S. agriculture flourish under the new regime of international agriculture, or will it decline as other U.S. industries have in the face of growing foreign competition?

In attempting to answer this question, it should be emphasized that the United States will remain a major agricultural producer at least in the short run because it possesses a large share of the world's arable land in the temperate zone. Few if any parts of the world can rival this fundamental source of U.S. comparative advantage in agriculture. But in view of recent experience in other industries, the United States would be ill advised to be complacent about the dominance of its agriculture in the longer run. Technological innovations that have been adopted in the United States are being adopted elsewhere. Just as the United States used mechanical innovations to complement its abundance of land and to substitute for its historical scarcity of labor, other countries are using technology to increase the productivity of their particular resource endowments.

Both history and logic tell us that as U.S. agriculture becomes integrated into world markets, it will continue to face technological and economic change. Such disequilibria can be viewed either as opportunities for economic gain or as disruptions of the status quo to be dealt with by government intervention and protectionist trade policy. The opening of the U.S. agricultural sector to trade implies continuing specialization and corresponding patterns of resource use. Producers who can be competitive in the international market stand to gain; those who cannot will face continuing competitive pressures from world markets. In a world of rapid technological change in both agricultural production and transportation, an increasing number of commodities are likely to become traded goods. Thus, in addition to the growing competition facing producers of commodities that are now traded, an increasing proportion of agricultural producers are likely to be participants in international markets.

These changes in agriculture have important implications for U.S. agricultural policy. First and foremost, agricultural policy must not inhibit the sector from adjusting to changes in technology and in

5

international markets. If U.S. policy is based on the view that disequilibria present opportunities for agricultural entrepreneurs, U.S. agriculture can flourish in the open economy environment. U.S. policy since the 1930s, however, has attempted (largely unsuccessfully) to protect farmers from variability of prices and incomes. The internationalization of agriculture means that present policies, based on a complex system of price supports, acreage controls, and production controls, will become increasingly outmoded and inappropriate for the problems facing agriculture. If the United States attempts to protect farmers from change, U.S. agriculture will inevitably decline as it fails to keep pace with changes in technology and international economic conditions. The problems that need to be addressed by agricultural policy in the 1980s and beyond are associated with a high rate of technological change in agriculture and increasing integration of the sector into world markets. Existing policies and the policy formation process are not designed to deal with these uncertainties and indeed may aggravate the sector's difficulties in adjusting to changing technology and world economic conditions.

The U.S. comparative advantage in major traded commodities, notably food and feed grains, means that a large segment of U.S. agriculture will be able to compete successfully in international markets. This optimistic statement requires strong caveats, however. A first is that the competitiveness of U.S. agricultural producers depends on both the domestic and the trade-related agricultural policies of the United States and other countries. Policy-induced distortions, such as production subsidies and price supports, can alter the international flow of traded commodities away from patterns implied by comparative advantage. A second caveat is that if the United States does move further in the direction of a market- and trade-oriented policy, U.S. producers that are neither domestically nor internationally competitive will be forced out of production.

The internationalization of agricultural production and trade means that agriculture will be increasingly under the influence of international trade policy. Trade policy and trade negotiations are likely to have major effects on the degree to which production and trade follow patterns implied by comparative advantage. As the internationalization of agriculture puts competitive pressure on segments of a country's agricultural sector, demands for protective measures will be made. The extent to which the international community can come to terms with these kinds of domestic and international issues will have much to do with the future of international agricultural trade and the future of major producing countries such as the United States.

Summary

The following points summarize the findings of this study.

First, the long-run trends in global economic growth, agricultural production, prices, and trade that have been observed over the past two decades are likely to be maintained. The developing countries will import more food from the developed countries, and the gradual long-run downward trend in international commodity prices will continue. The trends in production and prices from the mid-1980s to 2000 are likely to resemble those of the 1960s more than those of the 1970s. Technological change in agriculture and a transfer of resources out of agriculture will continue, especially in developing countries where high shares of the labor force are employed in agriculture.

Second, while the major long-run trends in production and prices of the past decades will continue, certain patterns seem likely to be accentuated. Notably, eastern Asia and Latin America are likely to continue to experience high rates of growth in per capita food production, and sub-Saharan Africa can be expected to continue to face stagnation or even reductions in per capita food production and real income. The net effect of these trends will be to increase further the volume of trade in agricultural commodities, especially cereals, between developed and developing countries.

Third, major shocks to the world markets are likely, which will generate large variations in world market conditions around the long-run trend. The kinds of market shocks that occurred in the 1970s and early 1980s are likely to recur. The presence of a small number of large actors in international commodity markets and the unpredictability of their behavior mean that major unanticipated policy changes are likely to continue to affect world commodity markets.

Fourth, the U.S. agricultural sector is undergoing a transition from an essentially closed economy in the 1950s to an increasing integration into world markets. Economic change in U.S. agriculture—formerly driven by domestic economic growth and technological change—will depend increasingly on the international economy. Because the United States possesses a strong comparative advantage in producing major traded agricultural commodities, it is likely to continue, over the long term, to be a major supplier of agricultural commodities to the rest of the world. But the continuing positive trend in productivity growth rates worldwide will lead to declines in real commodity prices that will drive increasing specialization of production throughout the world. Areas of marginal production will come under increasing pressure either to lower costs of production through technological change or to leave the industry.

Significant areas of relatively high-cost production in the United States are likely to face increasing competitive pressure from the highly productive regions of the world.

Fifth, technological change will remain a major force in U.S. and worldwide agriculture. The United States cannot expect to remain the only country with a highly modern, highly productive agriculture. Moreover, biogenetic research might lead to spectacular increases in productivity not only in the United States but throughout the world and in areas where conventional seed-fertilizer technology has not been suitable. Such changes, if they were to become widespread, would have profound effects on the structure of agriculture in the United States and around the world.

Sixth, agricultural policies of the United States and other major producers will play a significant role in the future of U.S. and world agriculture. Two extreme scenarios seem likely to bound the actual situation. One has the high price supports of the early 1980s continuing with acreage or output controls, combined with continued policies by the major producing countries to protect significant segments of their agricultures from foreign competition. A result would be to aggravate the existing distortions of U.S. and world production away from patterns implied by comparative advantage. Under this scenario the United States might continue to lose its export markets to other countries. The other scenario has the United States abandoning its policies of market intervention and letting world commodity markets set prices and output in the United States while the United States and other countries abandon their protective trade policies. Under this scenario, after an adjustment period, the United States would regain its export markets and play its rightful role as the major world supplier to importers of food and feed grains.

Note

1. Henry A. Wallace, *Our Debt and Duty to the Farmer* (New York: Century Publishing Co., 1925), chap. 12, "The Future of the American Farmer."

2
World Agricultural Development: An Introduction

Agricultural development is now generally recognized as an integral part of overall economic development. Modern economic development has been continuing throughout the world, in varying degrees and forms, since the industrial revolution began in England in the eighteenth century. The industrial revolution brought about fundamental changes in domestic and international markets that had profound effects on agricultural economies throughout the world. Although economic development has been a central concern of economists since the eighteenth century, not until the 1950s was the economic development of third world countries seriously scrutinized by Western scholars or politicians.

In the 1950s development economists tended to view agriculture as a poor relation in the grand scheme of economic development. They believed that economic development could occur only through large-scale investment in capital-intensive industries. According to this view, agriculture was a tradition-bound repository of "surplus labor," which could be transferred to the industrial sector without a loss of agricultural productivity. Moreover, since farmers' behavior was believed to be determined not by economic considerations but by tradition, it was reasoned that governments could finance general economic development in part by taxing agriculture—either directly by taxing production or indirectly through export policies and forced deliveries of goods to government marketing organizations—without affecting agricultural production.

The limited successes and frequent failures of capital-intensive schemes for economic development in third world countries led to a reexamination of economic development strategies in the 1960s. Economists began to recognize that agriculture's role in economic development was very different from the one in the surplus labor theory. They recognized that since underdeveloped economies were principally agricultural, agriculture was the major source of income and employment; thus the most logical means of promoting economic development was through investment in agriculture, not in industry. They also recognized that farm people, like people the world over, generally respond to economic incentives and that prices are as relevant to economic behavior in third world agricultures as elsewhere. And they recognized that the skills and knowledge of the vast majority of people in developing countries had to do with agriculture, not large-scale industry. Thus successful agricultural development came to be viewed as a necessary, perhaps a principal, component of economic development in third world countries.[1]

The social, economic, and political importance of agricultural development is underscored by the fact that a large part of the world's people—and the vast majority of the world's poorest people—earn their livelihood in agriculture. As Theodore W. Schultz has emphasized, to understand the problems of the very poor we need to understand the economics of agriculture.[2] Moreover, it has become increasingly apparent that third world agricultural development is likely to have important consequences for the agricultures of the more developed countries.

Predictions of high population growth rates have been a major reason for concern about third world economic development and its relation to agriculture. If those predictions are correct (and there are some good reasons to believe that many of them are overstated), they suggest that in the future vastly greater food production will be needed to feed the world. Some analysts have argued that to feed the world's population adequately, the developed countries must produce a large part of the world's food for export. According to this line of reasoning, policies that continue to promote production in developed countries such as the United States are justified despite current surpluses. At the same time continued and sometimes dramatic increases in food production have occurred in third world countries, as well as some serious failures.

The problem of feeding the world is often posed as the question whether agricultural production in third world countries will keep up with population growth in those countries. From an economic and policy point of view, however, that is not the most relevant issue, and its prominence in discussions of public policy has diverted attention from the fundamental economic and policy questions that are relevant. If each country were an autarky—an economic "island" economically independent of every other country—we could analyze the world food problem in terms of each country's production and consumption. But that surely is not the case. Since the economies of virtually all countries are becoming increasingly integrated into international markets, the relevant economic questions concern the efficient and equitable allocation of resources throughout the world so that the world can be supplied with the food it demands and needs. The relevant global policy questions concern how individual countries can contribute to or inhibit an efficient and equitable allocation of the world's resources.

Given the integration of individual countries into world agricultural markets, the important policy questions for the United States concern its role in world economic growth as third world countries develop and become increasingly involved in international markets. Some American agriculturalists have suggested, for example, that the U.S. policy of aiding agricultural development in third world countries is tantamount to subsidizing our competitors in agricultural markets.[3] They argue that if U.S. policy helps third world countries follow a development path similar to that followed by the Western countries, food production of third world countries might exceed the demands of their domestic population, and they might become serious agricultural competitors of the United States and other Western countries. Some economists argue, however, that this line of reasoning ignores the factors that affect the demand for U.S. agricultural products on world markets. To analyze these questions we need to understand the underlying economic factors that contribute to the world supply of agricultural products and demand for them.

Because agriculture is a major sector in the economies of developing countries, economic development has important consequences for agriculture, and conversely agricultural development has important effects on the world economy. This chapter examines these interrelations between third world economic development and agriculture.

What Is Economic Development?

Economic development is defined here as the process of capital accumulation, and capital is broadly defined as all assets—physical, human, social, and institutional—that create income and contribute to human welfare. Several observations are in order about this definition of economic development.

First, economic development requires investment in various categories of physical capital: the plant and equipment of private firms in manufacturing and agriculture, as well as such publicly held capital as transportation infrastructure and communications. Economic development also requires other kinds of changes, such as modifications

11

of social and institutional arrangements to facilitate capital accumulation and the creation of income. To the extent that such changes also require time and the use of real resources—that is, to the extent that they also impose real economic costs on society—it is useful to think of them as investments in social capital.

Economic development can be quantified in various ways. Data such as per capita gross domestic product (GDP) are often cited and interpreted as measures of the relative well-being or state of economic development of peoples in various countries or regions of the world (we shall see a great many such numbers in chapters 4 and 5). While such data do provide useful comparative information, they may be somewhat misleading because they fail to reflect the diversity of the phenomena involved in development. For example, GDP per capita was $238 in India in 1980 and $12,784 in the United States. These numbers suggest a staggering difference in economic well-being between the two countries. Yet this does not mean that India has not made substantial investments in various kinds of capital, physical as well as human and social.

To overcome the problems inherent in using per capita income to measure economic development, measures of the distribution of income and other measures of human welfare are often used. The United Nations collects information on education, life expectancy, infant mortality rates, housing, and sanitation for all countries. These data provide a broader view of economic development. In South Asia (India and the surrounding countries), life expectancy increased from thirty to forty-nine years from the 1930s to the 1960s despite rapid population growth. Similar progress has been seen in Africa and other parts of the third world. This positive change often contrasts with the picture derived from looking only at per capita GNP. This progress reflects changes in nutrition and health brought about by the introduction of modern medicine and sanitation practices and better diets and thus reflects investments in various forms of social capital.

Economic development must thus be defined not only by market income and physical capital accumulation but also by other dimensions of social and institutional change that enhance human welfare. These broader dimensions are much more difficult to measure than income and physical capital accumulation. As a practical matter, those more tangible aspects are typically quantified and used as indicators of development, but that does not mean that the less tangible or less easily quantified dimensions are less important. Indeed, in attempts to explain why one region develops and another does not, the intangibles—such as social norms and institutional arrangements—may be found to play an important role. If we ignore them simply because they are difficult to quantify, we may fail to understand the development process fully.

What Are the Causes of Economic Growth and Development?

The question of what causes economic growth has been asked at least since the eighteenth century, when Adam Smith published his famous treatise on the sources and causes of economic development, *The Wealth of Nations*.[4] According to the definition of development presented above, whatever factors generate the resources and incentives for capital accumulation cause economic growth and development. But what are those factors, and how do they operate? While it would be presumptuous to suggest that anyone knows the entire answer to these questions, we do know some factors that help us answer them.

Smith was one of the first economists to recognize the major importance in economic development of trade and the specialization in production that trade permits. In one remarkable chapter of his book, he observed that "the division of labor is limited by the extent of the market." Smith clearly understood that productivity gains from economies of scale and specialization in production are possible only insofar as firms have access to sufficiently large markets to support large-scale production. Thus the innovations in water, land, and air transport over the past centuries have all contributed significantly to economic development because of their effects on the extent of the market.

Perhaps of even greater importance than specialization in the twentieth century has been technological progress—the application of scientific knowledge to production so that more output can be obtained from a given bundle of resources. Technological progress was the source of the industrial revolution, and it is the source of the agricultural revolution that has profoundly affected agricultural production, especially since the 1950s.

Trade, specialization, and technological progress all lead to increased productivity, which provides both resources and incentives for the capital investment that is the basis of economic development. An important corollary is that underdevelopment is due to a lack of capital investment. In all cases of failed development, some reason must exist why the needed capital investment has not taken place.

It would be naive to believe that trade, specialization, and technological change occur in a social, institutional, and political vacuum. Indeed, an important issue is how noneconomic factors influence the economic and technological factors that lead to capital investment and development.

13

The Role of Agriculture in Economic Development

In the early stages of development agriculture plays an important role because most productive resources, both human and nonhuman, are in agriculture. In nonindustrial economies typically 90 percent or more of labor is employed in agriculture, and agricultural land and water supplies constitute the major natural resource. Most physical capital investment in such economies is in land—its clearing, leveling, and preparation for cultivation—and in livestock. Most human capital investment is in the informal training of children by their parents in the traditional agricultural knowledge that has been handed down for generations.

Because most productive resources are in agriculture at the beginning of economic development, resources must be transferred to other sectors of the economy as trade, specialization, and technological progress lead to economic growth.[5] In 1880 about 50 percent of male workers in the United States and about 80 percent in Japan were employed in agriculture; these percentages declined to less than 5 percent for the United States and less than 10 percent for Japan by 1970.

Fundamental economic forces drive the transition from a largely agricultural to a largely nonagricultural economy. As economic growth yields higher incomes, the demand for nonagricultural goods grows faster than the demand for agricultural goods. Producers of nonagricultural goods respond to the increased demands by bidding away resources (land, labor, capital) from agriculture and devoting them to nonagricultural production. The offer of higher wages in nonagricultural employment was one factor that led to the migration of labor out of agriculture in the United States and Japan.

The transition from "traditional" to "modern" agriculture is an important part of economic development. T. W. Schultz outlined this process in his seminal book *Transforming Traditional Agriculture*.[6] Contrary to the school of thought that viewed farmers in traditional agriculture as bound not by economic considerations but by social customs, Schultz argued that traditional agriculture is "poor but efficient." Farmers in traditional agriculture are efficient in the sense that they obtain as much as is possible from the resources at their disposal and their technology. But traditional agriculture is poor because of the low productivity of its resources and the resulting lack of economic incentives for capital accumulation.

Much research over the past two decades has produced evidence supporting Schultz's hypothesis. The implication for agriculture is that economic development cannot come about simply through more efficient use of the traditional technology and resources. Investments in agricultural research are needed to generate new technology that is more productive, and accompanying investments are needed in farmers' education, extension, and supporting infrastructure. The higher productivity that can be realized by farmers will provide the resources for capital investment and the incentive for farmers to invest.

Important elements of the development process are trade and specialization in production. Increased agricultural productivity leads to, and is caused by, increased specialization in agricultural production. But how does each country or region specialize? Economic theory tells us that each region specializes in the products in which it has a *comparative advantage,* that is, those that it can produce *relatively* more efficiently than its trading partners (note that the key factor is the cost of producing one good relative to the cost of producing another, not the absolute costs of production). Agriculture specializes according to each region's climate and resource base, as those factors determine the commodities in which it is relatively most productive.

Moreover, given a region's resource endowment, the relative scarcity of factors of production (land, labor, capital) influences the kinds of technological innovation that are most useful. This influence of relative prices on technological innovation is the basis of the theory of *induced innovation.* The United States and Japan again provide useful examples of the specialization in production and induced innovation that have occurred in response to each country's resource endowment. Land has been more abundant and labor scarcer in the United States than in Japan. The United States thus has a comparative advantage in producing land-intensive products such as grain crops and livestock. In contrast, Japan has a comparative advantage in rice, vegetables, and other crops that can be cultivated with a very high labor intensity. Consequently, the United States has developed and adopted mechanical and biological technology that exploits its great land endowment; Japan has relied primarily on biological technology, such as fertilizer-responsive varieties, that saves land and is complementary to its labor-intensive agriculture.[7]

The Role of Population Growth

The past several decades have seen unprecedented growth in world population, largely in the poorest parts of the world. World population increased from about 2.5 billion in 1950 to 4.4 billion in 1980. This growth occurred at the same time that other economic and social problems, such as degradation of the environment, exhaustion of natural resources, and rapid urban growth, began to be recognized.

15

Many, if not all, of these problems have been widely viewed as due largely to excessive population growth. Some world economic models even raised the specter of widespread famine and economic disaster if population growth and the attendant environmental deterioration were not immediately curtailed.[8] In response to these extremely dire predictions of economic collapse due to population growth, the opposite extreme position has been put forward—that population growth is economically and socially desirable.[9] In view of the role capital investment plays in development, to understand this issue we need to know how population growth is related to capital accumulation. Appeal to economic theory and recent experience in developing countries suggest reasons why population may have both positive and negative effects on capital investment. Thus reality seems likely to lie between the two extreme views of the effects of population growth.[10]

A high rate of population growth may have positive effects on economic development for at least one reason: labor is a basic factor of production, and a larger population might mean a more abundant supply of the labor needed for production and investment.. But a growing population also imposes real costs on society, in consumption, education, and public investments in infrastructure for transportation, drinking water, and sewage disposal. If the demand for these goods grows faster than society's ability to provide them, the collective welfare of society may decline.

Some demographers and others have treated population as a factor determined largely outside the economic system. Malthus's theory that population will grow exponentially until limited by the scarcity of food was based on a view of population as a purely biological phenomenon. A related view underlies many of the recent studies of population growth, which predict exponential rates of growth into the next century with devastating consequences for third world countries, perhaps for all of humanity.

The population growth of the 1950–1980 period appears to have been due to the increased availability of modern medicine, improved sanitation, and food. Consequently, many of the very poor regions of the world have experienced declining infant mortality rates and longer life expectancy. But the population growth rate seems to have peaked in most regions; although world population will continue to rise, it will probably not do so at the rate seen in recent decades. The World Bank reports that the population growth rate in low-income countries averaged about 2 percent from 1973 to 1980 and projects a decline to 1.8 percent over the 1980–2000 period. In contrast, in the

16

industrial market countries the corresponding numbers are 0.7 and 0.4 percent.

There are several reasons to believe that the effects of population on economic development have been overstated and that the predictions of continued population growth at disastrous rates are not likely to be correct. First, it is fallacious to infer that population growth caused various economic and social problems simply because it preceded them. Recent studies indicate that urban growth is a function not so much of population growth as of government policies that encourage people to move to cities. Similarly, many of the environmental problems in evidence around the world are due not to population growth but to economic growth.

The proposition that population growth is biologically determined and does not depend on economic factors has been subjected to serious criticism. Recent research suggests that, on the contrary, population is influenced by economic factors such as income, the costs of bearing and raising children, and the contribution of children to family income. Many studies have found that as incomes increase, the economic benefits of children decrease, and the costs of having children increase.[11] Thus the process of development generally has a negative effect on population growth. As development proceeds, an automatic economic mechanism tends to counteract other factors, such as improved hygiene and diet, that increase fertility and decrease infant mortality. These changes take place relatively slowly over multiple generations, and it is difficult to observe them in short periods.

In view of these observations, it seems fair to say that although population growth does play a role in economic development, its importance has been overstated. Its effects must be evaluated in the context of the other major forces affecting capital accumulation.

Concluding Comments

We have learned a great deal in the past several decades about third world economic development and its consequences for agriculture. We now understand that the low incomes of farmers in less-developed countries are due to the low productivity of their resources and technologies. The lack of capital investment reflects a lack of investment opportunities. To achieve higher productivity, more productive technologies and the accompanying capital investment are needed. Basic and applied agricultural research is required to generate new technologies adapted to the local environment. Government

FIGURE 1

The Production Possibilities Frontier and Demand Functions

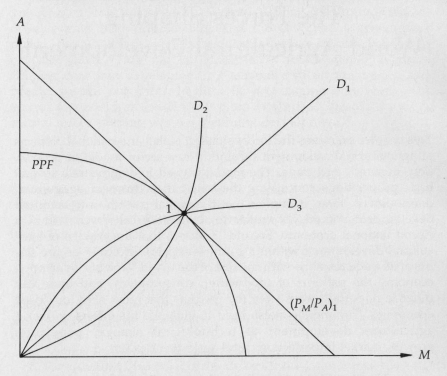

addition, the technology changes over time.[2] The production possibilities frontier *(PPF)* corresponding to this technology is shown in figure 1.

Given consumers' preferences for the aggregate commodities A and M, their prices, and aggregate income Y, the aggregate demand function defines the quantities demanded of each commodity.[3] The demand side of the economy is represented by the demand function D_1. Each point on this curve corresponds to the commodity quantities demanded at a particular income and price combination, and movements along the curve show the effects on demand of changing incomes with prices held constant.[4] The *PPF* and the demand function D_1 can be combined to determine the economy's equilibrium. In equilibrium the economy must be on its *PPF*, and prices must be such that the resulting production of A and M just satisfies aggregate demand at aggregate income $Y = P_A A + P_M M$. This equilibrium condition is achieved at point 1, where the aggregate preference function

U (or utility function) is tangent to the *PPF*. The equilibrium relative commodity price at that point, $(P_M/P_A)_1$, is equal to the slope of these curves at their tangency.[5] The equilibrium real income level for each commodity is defined by the intercepts of the price line that intersects the equilibrium point 1 at the equilibrium prices.

One fundamental economic force driving economic development is consumers' demand for commodities in response to income changes. An important fact is that the income-share-weighted sum of the income elasticities over all commodities is equal to unity. In the case of two aggregate commodities, it follows immediately from the budget constraint that

$$s_A \epsilon_A + s_M \epsilon_M = 1$$

where $s_A = P_A A/Y$ and $s_M = P_M M/Y$ are the income shares of A and M and ϵ_A and ϵ_M are the corresponding income elasticities of demand. In the two-commodity case, there are three possibilities for the relation between income elasticities: $\epsilon_A = \epsilon_M = 1$; $\epsilon_A > 1 > \epsilon_M$; or $\epsilon_A < 1 < \epsilon_M$.

These conditions on the income elasticities of demand imply some important restrictions on the shape of the aggregate commodity demand function. In particular, it is known that all income elasticities are unity if and only if consumer preferences (the utility function) exhibit the property that the income expansion path of the demand function is linear, as D_1 is in figure 1.[6] If this condition does not hold, the expansion path will not be linear. D_2 shows the case where $\epsilon_A > 1 > \epsilon_M$ at all income levels; D_3 shows the case where $\epsilon_M > 1 > \epsilon_A$ at all income levels.

It is well documented that food, as an aggregate, has a lower income elasticity than other commodities (this empirical fact is known as Engel's law). It follows that in a two-good aggregate world, the income elasticity of demand for agricultural products as a group is less than unity and the elasticity for M is greater than unity. These elasticities imply that the aggregate commodity demand function generates an income expansion path like D_3. This simple property of demand behavior has profound effects on the long-term character of economic development, as we shall see.

Income growth in modern times has been due primarily to technological change, that is, the application of scientific knowledge to the production of real goods and services. Since there is no compelling theoretical reason to believe that technological change occurs systematically faster in one sector of the economy than in another, it will be assumed that technological change is *output neutral*, that is, that the

21

FIGURE 2

Technological Change in a Closed Economy

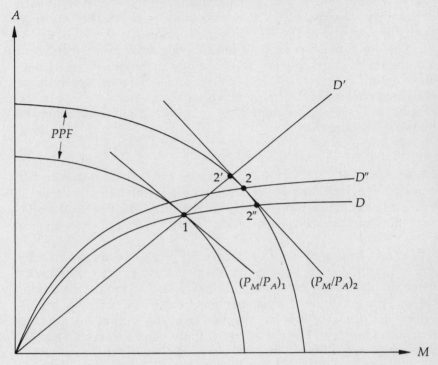

PPF shifts as in figure 2 so that its slope along any ray from the origin is constant.[7] Consequently, the line tangent to the PPF at point 1 is equal to the line tangent to the PPF at point 2'.

We can now combine the demand and the supply sides of the economy to examine the pattern of economic development that will occur in response to technological change. As the PPF shifts out because of technological change, real aggregate income increases, that is, more of both A and M can be obtained by consumers at a given relative commodity price ratio. Indeed, if both income elasticities were unity, the demand function would be represented by D', and the new equilibrium after a period of growth would occur at the intersection of the PPF and D' at point 2', where the same equilibrium commodity prices hold as at point 1. Since we know that the income elasticity for M is greater than unity, however, and that the income elasticity for A is less than unity, the demand function must be shaped like D. If at point 2" the slope of the PPF were the same as at point 1, the general equilibrium of the economy would occur there. Because the technological change is output neutral, the slope at point 2″ must be greater (in absolute terms) than at point 2′. Given the structure of consumer preferences, the new equilibrium point 2 must lie between points 2′ and 2″, so that $(P_M/P_A)_2 > (P_M/P_A)_1$. Note that the change in equilibrium prices causes the demand function to shift from D to $D″$.

The equilibrium price of M must rise in relation to the price of A to induce the relatively faster growth in production of M demanded by consumers as their incomes increase. The movement from point 1 to point 2 corresponds to an increase in production of both A and M. Yet because M must increase faster than A, the share of national income created in the A sector declines. Thus, under output-neutral technological change and unequal income elasticities, *economic growth induces relative decline in the sector whose income elasticity is less than unity.* Throughout the world the declining sector has been agriculture.

This pattern of economic development has equally profound effects on the use of productive resources. Given fixed stocks of the aggregate inputs L and C, it follows that the demand for resources in the more rapidly growing sector is likely to increase at a higher rate. This induces a factor market disequilibrium characterized by an increase in the wages of labor and the rental rate on capital in the more rapidly growing sector relative to the other sector. Thus resources are drawn out of A and into M to facilitate the more rapid growth of M than of A.

To illustrate this change in factor markets, suppose further that technological change in each sector is *factor neutral*, that is, at given factor prices the use of factors changes proportionally. Because of the increase in P_M relative to P_A, the demand for inputs increases more for M than for A. Figure 3 illustrates these changes in the labor market. The horizontal axis measures the total labor force, with the employment in A measured from left to right and in M from right to left; the vertical axis measures the wage rate. Early in the development process, when income is relatively low, more labor is employed in agriculture, as at point L_1 and wage rate W_1. Technological change increases the demand for resources in both sectors, but the increase in P_M/P_A causes factor demand to increase more in M than in A. Consequently, the new equilibrium in the labor market occurs at point 2, where labor has moved from A to M at a higher real wage. This analysis of the factor markets illustrates another fundamental implication of the growth model: *with input-neutral and output-neutral technological change, employment in the sector with the low income elasticity declines both relatively and absolutely.*

In summary, in an aggregate two-sector growth model of a closed economy, neutral technological change combined with an income

FIGURE 3

Effects of Technological Change on the Labor Market

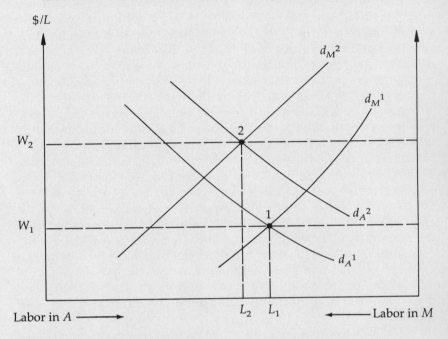

$/L

Labor in A ⟶ L_2 L_1 ⟵ Labor in M

elasticity of demand for manufactured goods higher than for agricultural goods leads to a distinct pattern of economic development. This development path is marked by a *relative* decline in the agricultural sector as measured by the share of national income it generates and by a *relative and absolute* decline in resource use in agriculture.

How relevant are these conclusions to a world not characterized by neutral technological change? Note first that, historically, a high rate of technological change of the sort associated with modern economic growth has tended to occur earlier in the manufacturing sector than in the agricultural sector. Working through the preceding analysis, we can see that technological change biased toward the manufacturing sector reinforces the results derived under the neutrality assumption. In contemporary less-developed countries (LDCs), however, agriculture has access to as much modern technology as manufacturing; so it is more reasonable to assume that technological change is output neutral. If the induced-innovation theory is valid, technological change will be input biased in the same direction in both sectors of developing economies. Since firms in both sectors face the same relative factor prices, they perceive an incentive to adopt

24

innovations that save the relatively scarce resource. Consequently, the pattern of relative changes in factor demands is likely to be the same in the case of input-biased technological change as in the input-neutral case. The conclusions derived from the assumption of neutral technical change will be valid unless technical change bias in agriculture is sufficiently labor-using and in manufacturing is strongly labor-saving.

The Two-Sector Growth Model for an Open Economy

This section explores the implications of the two-sector growth model in a "small" or price-taking economy open to international trade in commodities in competitive world markets. For the time being I abstract from the possibility that a country might possess monopoly power in world commodity markets or that its government might intervene in trade. This simple model is useful for discovering the fundamental economic forces driving patterns of production and resource use during economic development. Later I will introduce and discuss monopoly power and government intervention in world trade.

The discussion begins with the closed economy model of the previous section. Opening a small, price-taking economy to trade means that consumers and producers face international market prices for both agricultural and manufactured products. Figure 4 shows the effects on consumption and production before economic growth occurs. The initial equilibrium is at point 1 and corresponding commodity prices $(P_M/P_A)_1$. The world price of A is higher relative to the price of M, as indicated by a flatter price line $(P_M/P_A)_w$. This situation is representative of an agricultural developing country.

At the world commodity prices firms produce at point 1' in equilibrium. This country is thus revealed as having a comparative advantage in producing agricultural commodities and can consume more of both A and M by producing more A and less M and trading A for M in world markets. At world prices the demand function shifts from D to D', and the budget line rotates around the PPF so that with income generated by production at point 1', consumers can consume at point 1". The "gains from trade" are thus the increased utility consumers obtain as the economy moves from consuming at point 1 to consuming at point 1".

Now introduce into the analysis economic growth due to output-neutral technological change. As the PPF curve shifts out, production increases along the expansion path $0E$, at the constant world commodity prices. In contrast to the closed economy model, domestic

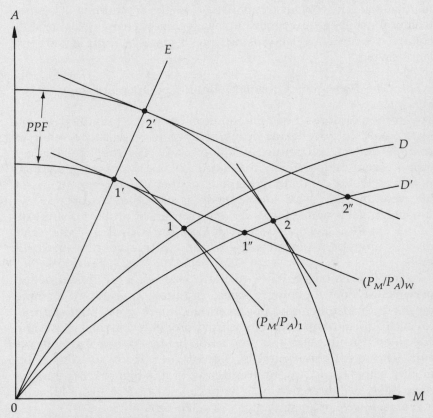

FIGURE 4

Technological Change in an Open Economy

production is independent of domestic demand and depends on the country's resource endowment, its technology, and world commodity prices. Consumption moves from point 1″ to 2″ along the demand function D'. Demand is now unconstrained by the domestic production technology and depends only on preferences, income, and world prices.

The model demonstrates that an open economy will exhibit different patterns of consumption, production, and resource use from those of a closed economy. Even though the income elasticity of demand for M exceeds that of demand for A, the economy's domestic equilibrium does not force increased domestic production of M relative to production of A because production patterns are independent of domestic consumption patterns. In the case of output-neutral technical change both sectors' production grows at the same rate, and

26

there is no change in either sector's contribution to national income. The pattern of input employment is determined by both output and input biases in technological change. If technical change is also input neutral, wages and capital rental rates are bid up at the same rate in both sectors. There is no change in either the relative or the absolute levels of employment of the two sectors. Different patterns of input-biased technological change in the sectors would lead to different patterns of resource use, with factors moving from the factor-saving sector to the factor-using sector in response to factor price changes.

In summary, when the small country two-sector growth model is opened to trade, production decisions depend on technology, resource endowments, and world prices; consumption depends on income, world prices, and consumers' preferences. Domestic production and consumption need not be equated in equilibrium as they must be in a closed economy. Differences between production and consumption are accommodated through international trade.

Capital Investment and Population Growth

In chapter 2 economic development was defined as the process of capital accumulation. Yet thus far growth in the two-sector model has been described in terms of technological change alone. This can indeed be the case when gains in efficiency are obtained from *disembodied technological change*, that is, from new methods of using existing labor and capital more productively. In most cases, however, technological change is in part *embodied* in new forms of capital (both human capital in the form of knowledge and skills and nonhuman capital in the form of machines, new seed varieties, and so forth).

In very general terms, capital investment can be thought of as forgone consumption in the present to obtain more consumption in the future. In the two-sector model the production possibilities frontier can be thought of as representing output net of capital investment. Then by dating the outputs M and A, we would see smaller amounts of M and A available for consumption or trade in one period but a correspondingly greater shift of the PPF in future periods because of the capital investment. For purposes of this analysis, the shifts of the PPF can be interpreted as reflecting the effects of both the technological change and the corresponding capital investment required for its implementation.

Population growth can be represented in the model along lines similar to those for capital investment. To obtain an additional member of the labor force, both individuals and society as a whole must sacrifice current consumption to obtain a greater stock of human

27

FIGURE 6

A Production Subsidy in a Large Open Economy

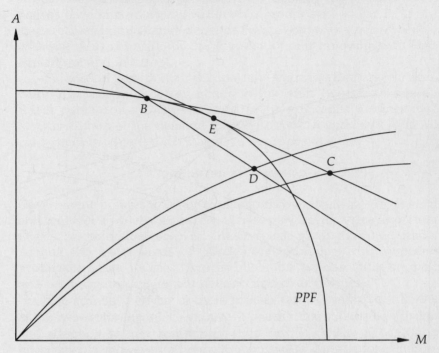

without intervention produces at point *E* and consumes at point *C*. Restricting agricultural output to point *B* drives down the relative price P_M/P_A and moves the consumption point to *D*, allowing the country to be better off by consuming more of both *A* and *M* because of the improved terms of trade. This is the essence of its monopoly power. While this argument seems valid if the country has absolute monopoly power, it is rare in the longer run that other producers will not enter the market in response to the increased price of agricultural commodities. If this happens, the price declines toward its original level. The country restricting its output sees its terms of trade deteriorate and its consumption move to a point such as *D'*. At this point the country is worse off than before the policy. Moreover, if the country were then to eliminate its output control policy and the new entrants into the supply side of the market remained in production, the world equilibrium price would be lower than it was before the output control policy was implemented. Thus the net effect of this sequence of policies would be a deteriorated terms of trade (a lower relative price

FIGURE 7

Output Control in a Large Open Economy

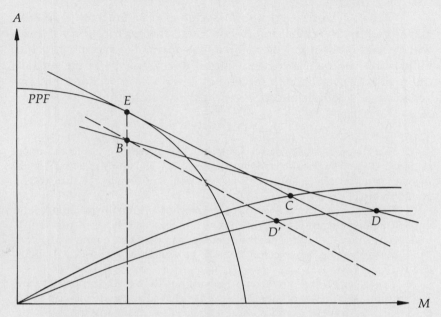

of its exported good), and the country would still be worse off than before it implemented the policy.[10]

The World Model

Consider now the world economy composed of a large number of countries of the kind described in the preceding section. In this section this collection of countries is aggregated into worldwide sectors representing agriculture and manufacturing, and all consumers are likewise aggregated. Thus the world as a whole is viewed as a "closed economy," as indeed it will be until the day of interplanetary trade arrives.

It should be apparent that the analysis of the closed economy can be transferred directly to the aggregate world economy. Under the same set of assumptions it follows that the pattern of economic development described there should hold for the world economy as a whole. Agriculture must decline in relation to manufacturing in its contribution to world income, and resources must be transferred from agriculture to manufacturing. Yet total agricultural output grows (as long as agricultural commodities are not an inferior good). These implications of the model can be verified with available data, and I shall do so in chapter 4.

When the world agricultural sector is disaggregated, the particular pattern of agricultural development that each country follows will depend on its domestic comparative advantage and other factors influencing the pattern of agricultural development. These include the extent of government intervention, market imperfections, and the government's policies affecting technological change.

Notes

1. This chapter's analysis uses assumptions deemed relevant to an understanding of global agricultural development. See texts on international trade theory for exhaustive treatment of all possible permutations of the model's assumptions.

2. The aggregate technology can be represented formally in terms of the implicit aggregate production function $F [A, M, L, C] = 0$. The function is indexed by time, t, to represent the effects of technological change.

3. The aggregate demand function can be written as an implicit function $D[Y, P_A, P_M, A, M] = 0$.

4. D_1 is referred to as an income expansion path in the commodity space. It corresponds to the set of values of A and M that solve the demand function $D[Y, P_A, P_M, A, M] = 0$ as Y varies and P_A and P_M are held constant. Note that holding income constant and changing prices would shift the curve to a different position in figure 1.

5. Formally, the equilibrium relative commodity price is defined as $P_M / P_A = -MRT_{A,M} = -MRS_{A,M}$, where MRT is the marginal rate of transformation along the PPF (the slope of the PPF at a point) and MRS is the marginal rate of substitution along the utility function (the slope of the utility function at a point).

6. This property is known as homotheticity of the utility function.

7. This concept of output-neutral technological change can be more formally defined as $\partial MRT_{A,M} / \partial t = 0$. For further discussion of this concept, see Susan M. Capalbo and John M. Antle, *Agricultural Productivity: Measurement and Explanation* (Washington, D.C.: Resources for the Future, 1988), chap. 2.

8. See U.S. Department of Agriculture, *Food Policies in Developing Countries*, Foreign Agricultural Economics Report no. 194, 1983.

9. Malcolm D. Bale and Ernst Lutz, *Price Distortions in Agriculture and Their Effects: An International Comparison*, World Bank Staff Working Paper no. 359, 1979.

10. For a further discussion of this phenomenon of irreversibility in agricultural supply, see John M. Antle and R. E. Howitt, "Agricultural Resources in an Open Economy," in John Sutton, ed., *Agricultural Trade and Natural Resources: Discovering the Critical Linkages* (Boulder, Colo.: Lynne Reinner Publishers, 1988).

4
World Agricultural Development, 1960–1980

This chapter examines the record of agricultural development since 1960 through major trends in key variables identified in chapter 3. I begin with an examination of world and regional data to verify the implications of the two-sector growth model discussed in chapter 3. The rest of the chapter summarizes the postwar data on population and vital statistics, regional development performance, and agricultural research and development.

World Data

Tables 1 and 2 present data on aggregate production, agricultural production, and labor in agriculture for the world, the developed countries, and the less-developed countries (LDCs) for 1960 through 1983. These data tell us a number of important facts about the changes that took place in the world's agricultures.

Total real production more than doubled from 1960 to 1980 in the world as a whole and in the developed countries and more than tripled in the LDCs. The LDCs' real product increased from less than one-fifth of the developed countries' in 1960 to one-quarter by 1975. Thus while the LDCs as a group remain far below the developed countries in absolute standard of living, they have achieved substantial absolute improvements.

The world's agricultural product declined from about 11 percent of total product in 1960 to 7 percent by 1980. Thus, as the model of chapter 3 predicted, with economic growth the relative importance of agriculture in aggregate product declined. Similarly, the share of labor employed in agriculture in the world declined to about 45 percent in 1980 from 58 percent in 1960, as the world two-sector model predicts.

Throughout the period the percentage of real output in agriculture in the developed countries was low; it declined from 5.7 to 3 percent over the period. In contrast, the share of LDC real output that came from agriculture was one-third in 1960 but declined to about

TABLE 1

VALUE OF PRODUCTION AND SHARES OF PRODUCTION AND LABOR IN AGRICULTURE, THE WORLD, DEVELOPED COUNTRIES, AND LESS-DEVELOPED COUNTRIES, 1960–1983

	Gross National Product (billions of 1983 dollars)			Gross Domestic Product in Agriculture (percent)			Labor in Agriculture (percent)		
	World	Developed countries	LDCs	World	Developed countries	LDCs	World	Developed countries	LDCs
1960	5,350	3,460	620	11	5.7	33.8	57.7	20.2	71.4
1965	6,850	4,470	840	10	5.0	31.0	54.2	23.4	69.4
1970	8,800	5,580	1,160	9[a]	4.1	23.5	51.3	18.5	66.3
1975	10,700	6,490	1,630	9[a]	5[a]	26[a]	48.4	15.2	62.9
1980	12,700	7,680	2,130	7	4	20	45.3	12.5	59.2
1981	13,000	7,830	2,160	7	3	19	44.7	12.0	58.4
1982	13,000	7,790	2,180	7	3	19	44.1	11.6	57.6
1983	13,300	7,970	2,190	—	—	—	43.6	11.1	56.9

a. 1973.

SOURCES: Labor statistics from Food and Agriculture Organization, *FAO Production Yearbook* (Rome: FAO), vols. 29, 30, 36, 38. GNP figures from CIA Directorate of Intelligence, *Handbook of Economic Statistics, 1984,* September 1984. Percentage of GDP in agriculture from World Bank, "International Capital and Economic Development, World Development Indicators," *World Development Report, 1985* (Washington, D.C.: World Bank, 1985); and World Bank, *World Tables, 1984, 1985.*

TABLE 2
WORLD POPULATION AND FOOD PRODUCTION, 1960–1985

	Population (millions)	Food Production (cereals plus meat)	
		Total (millions of metric tons)	Per capita (kilograms)
World			
1960	2,986	1,031	345
1965	3,334	1,090	327
1970	3,694	1,319	357
1975	4,076	1,501	368
1980	4,449	1,700	382
1982	4,605	1,840	400
1985	4,837	1,989	411
Developed economies			
1960	963	407	422
1965	1,025	401	391
1970	1,074	689	641
1975	1,125	771	685
1980	1,169	886	758
1982	1,185	960	810
1985	1,210	1,013	837
Developing economies			
1960	2,023	309	152
1965	2,309	356	154
1970	2,620	630	240
1975	2,953	730	247
1980	3,281	814	248
1982	3,420	880	257
1985	3,626	976	269

SOURCE: Food and Agriculture Organization, *FAO Production Yearbook*, vols. 15, 19, 29, 34, 39.

one-fifth by the 1980s. Similar patterns hold for the labor force in agriculture.

In addition to providing empirical support for the two-sector growth model, these data provide important information on the absolute growth in agricultural output in the developed and developing countries. Real world agricultural production rose from about $346 billion in U.S. dollars in 1960 to about $550 billion by the early 1980s, a more than 50 percent increase even though the *share* of agriculture in total output declined. In the LDCs real agricultural product increased by over 100 percent, from about $200 billion in 1960 to over $400 billion in the 1980s. Thus the share of world agricultural output accounted for by the LDCs increased from about 60 percent to more than 70 percent during a twenty-year period. Although the LDCs have a much lower total real product than the developed countries, they produce a large and growing proportion of the world's agricultural output.

Population and Vital Statistics

In the early 1960s the rate of population growth worldwide was estimated at 2 percent, a rate that would double the population in thirty-five years.[1] Low-income countries were contributing disproportionately to the high growth rate because of a combination of traditionally high fertility rates, a rapid reduction in infant mortality rates, and an increase in life expectancy attributable to improvements in public sanitation and medical services. These factors continued in the 1980s to lead to much higher population growth rates in the less-developed parts of the world (table 3). The world population increased from about 3.0 billion in 1960 to about 4.5 billion by 1980. The population predictions of the early 1960s are proving to be quite accurate.

Although world population grew at unprecedented rates in the 1960–1980 period, marked improvements also occurred in living conditions and the "quality" of the population as indicated by vital statistics and educational attainment. Infant mortality fell significantly, for example, in Africa, Asia, and Latin America, although Africa continues to have the highest rate. In literacy Africa again falls far short of Asia or Latin America, but all three regions showed substantial improvement.

Although population growth rates remain high, especially in the poorest parts of the world, there are indications that they are beginning to fall. I return to this point in the next chapter.

Regional Development Performance

The data of table 4 show sustained growth in all the less-developed regions in total real product and a steady decline in the shares of agriculture in real output and of the labor force in agriculture since 1960. Substantial regional differences appear in relative shares of output and labor in agriculture.

Although sub-Saharan Africa's total agricultural output increased over the period, this growth came not primarily from technological change but from increases in acreage and labor input. In contrast, Asia's and Latin America's growth in real agricultural output was due

36

TABLE 3
Population and Vital Statistics, by Region, 1950–1985

	Midyear Population (millions)							Annual Rate of Increase (percent)		Infant Mortality (per 1,000 births)		Literacy (percent)		Life Expectancy at Birth (years)	
	1950	1960	1965	1970	1975	1980	1984	1960–65	1980–85	1950–55	1980–85	1960	1981	1950–55	1980–85
Africa	222	278	314	357	410	476	537	2.48	3.0	182	114	19.0	40	37.3	49.7
North America	166	199	214	227	239	252	251	1.49	0.9	29	12	97.6	99	69.0	74.1
Latin America	165	217	249	284	322	362	397	2.80	2.3	126	63	67.5	79	51.2	64.1
Asia	1,366	1,666	1,853	2,095	2,357	2,591	2,777	2.15	1.7	153	87	45.0	63	39.4	57.9
Europe	392	425	445	459	474	484	490	0.91	0.3	62	16	94.7	97	65.4	73.2
Oceania	13	16	17	19	21	23	24	2.08	1.5	68	39	88.5	90	60.7	67.6
Soviet Union	180	214	231	242	253	265	276	1.49	1.0	73	25	94.7	97	61.7	70.9
World	2,504	3,015	3,323	3,683	4,076	4,453	4,752	1.99	1.7	138	n.a.	60.7	70	47.0	n.a.

n.a. = not available.

Sources: United Nations Department of International Economic and Social Affairs (Statistical Office), *Demographic Yearbook, 1984* (New York, 1986); *World Population Prospects, Estimates and Projection as Assessed in 1982*, Population Studies no. 86 (New York, 1985); *World Population Prospects, Estimates and Projection as Assessed in 1980*, Population Studies no. 78 (New York, 1981); and *World Statistics in Brief*, Statistical Papers series 5, nos. 2, 8 (New York, 1977, 1983).

TABLE 4: Value of Production and Shares of Production and Labor in Agriculture, Less-Developed Countries, by Region, 1960–1980

	GDP (millions of 1975 dollars) (per capita in parentheses)			GDP in Agriculture (percent)					Labor in Agriculture (percent)			
	Africa	Latin America	Asia	Sub-Saharan Africa	North Africa	Latin America	East Asia	South Asia	Africa	Latin America	East Asia	South Asia
1960	34,600 (124)	69,700 (321)	67,600	36.1	24.1	16.4	45.6	48.9	80.5	47.8	74.2	69.1
1965	—	—	—	32.8	23.2	15.8	52.5	45.6	78.1	44.2	70.9	65.5
1970	76,500 (214)	163,400 (575)	123,700 (108)	27.6	19.8	12.2	27.6	46.1	75.5	40.8	68.2	61.1
1975	187,800 (458)	349,500 (1,085)	244,700 (190)	—	—	12.0	—	—	72.5	37.3	65.4	57.1
1978	275,500 (778)	510,100 (1,462)	374,900 (269)	—	—	11.6	—	—	70.5	35.4	63.5	55.4
1979	326,500 (894)	637,800 (1,777)	432,300 (303)	—	—	11.2	—	—	69.9	34.7	62.9	54.6
1980	421,300 (885)	824,100 (2,276)	513,400 (355)	31.3a	11.6a	10.1a	26.4a	36.1a	69.1	33.9	62.2	53.0

a. 1981.

SOURCES: Percentage of GDP in agriculture from World Bank, *World Tables*, vol. 1, *Economic Data* (Baltimore: Johns Hopkins University Press, 1983); World Bank, *World Tables* (Baltimore: Johns Hopkins University Press, 1976); and Economic Commission for Latin America, *Statistical Yearbook for Latin America*, 1980. Percentage of labor in agriculture from FAO, *FAO Production Yearbook* (Rome, 1985), vols. 29, 31, 34, 38. GDP from Department of International Economic and Social Affairs, Statistical office, UN, *Statistical Yearbook* (New York, 1983); UN, *Yearbook of National Account Statistics, 1981* (New York, 1983), vol. 11, *International Tables*; and UN, *Yearbook of National Account Statistics, 1978* (New York, 1979), vol. 11, *International Tables*.

more to growth in yields. Clearly, sub-Saharan Africa has had much less success than other parts of the developing world in achieving technological advance in agriculture.

These regional differences are also apparent in the data on population growth and major food crop production presented in table 5. The 1960–1980 period saw a considerable growth rate for all LDCs (3.1 percent), but the high population growth rate meant that per capita growth was a modest 0.7 percent. The high degree of aggregation obscures the diversity among regions, however. China attained a very high growth rate of over 4 percent and a relatively low 2.1 percent population growth rate; East and Southeast Asia had a 3.1 percent growth rate of food production and a 0.7 percent per capita rate. Central Africa, lower South America, and Mexico and Central America had similar patterns of growth. Upper South America and South Asia did considerably worse in per capita terms because of high population growth rates, despite quite high rates of production growth. The remaining parts of Africa and the Middle East experienced declines in per capita food production due to relatively low production growth and the highest population growth rates in the world.

Table 6 shows the patterns of production growth in the major LDC regions. Overall, 87 percent of the increase in major food crops was in cereals, and the major regions of the world matched this pattern except for sub-Saharan Africa, where only 55 percent of increased production was in cereals. Sub-Saharan Africa performed worse than any other part of the developing world absolutely and particularly per hectare.

A more detailed picture of the differences in sources of production growth is presented in table 7, which breaks down growth in food production into components attributable to increases in acreage and those attributable to increases in yield.[2] The LDCs achieved growth in food production primarily through a growth in yield that can be attributed to technological change. While Asia performed very well and Latin America reasonably well in increasing yields, parts of Africa, especially sub-Saharan Africa, performed very poorly. West Africa and Central Africa actually experienced declines in yield, and all of their output growth was attributable to increases in acreage.

Table 8 presents data on consumption of basic food staples as food and as animal feed. This distinction is important because grains for direct human consumption have a very low income elasticity and meat and feed have much higher income elasticities, often near or exceeding unity.[3] In most parts of the world food staples are used more for food than for feed, and this pattern has not changed mark-

39

TABLE 5: POPULATION AND MAJOR FOOD CROP PRODUCTION, BY REGION AND SUBREGION, 1980, AND AVERAGE ANNUAL GROWTH RATES, 1961–1980

	Population			Major Food Crop Production			
	1980 (millions)	1980 (percent)	1961–80 annual growth rate (percent)	Quantity, 1980 (millions of metric tons)	1980 (percent)	1961–80 annual growth rate (percent)	1961–80 per capita growth rate (percent)
Developing countries	3,273	100	2.4	841.9	100	3.1	0.7
(Excluding China)	(2,270)	(69)	(2.5)	(543.1)	(65)	(2.6)	(0.1)
Asia	2,325	71	2.3	593.8	70	3.4	1.1
(Excluding China)	(1,322)	(40)	(2.4)	(295.0)	(35)	(2.8)	(0.4)
China	1,003	31	2.1	198.9	35	4.1	2.0
South Asia	880	27	2.4	184.8	22	2.7	0.3
East and Southeast Asia	442	13	2.4	110.2	13	3.1	0.7
North Africa and Middle East	253	8	2.7	68.0	8	2.5	-0.2
Northern Africa	108	3	2.6	21.1	2	2.3	-0.3
Western Asia	145	5	2.8	46.9	6	2.6	-0.2
Sub-Saharan Africa	338	10	2.8	72.4	9	1.7	-1.1
West Africa	148	4	2.9	32.7	4	0.8	-2.1
Central Africa	59	2	2.3	12.1	2	2.9	0.6
Eastern and southern Africa	131	4	3.0	27.6	3	2.4	-0.6
Latin America	357	11	2.6	107.7	13	2.8	0.2
Mexico and Central America	117	4	2.9	29.7	3	3.4	0.5
Upper South America	198	6	2.7	55.6	7	2.8	0.1
Lower South America	42	1	1.6	22.4	3	2.3	0.7

SOURCE: Leonardo A. Paulino, *Food in the Third World* (Washington, D.C.: International Food Policy Research Institute, 1986).

edly in the 1966–1980 period. Latin America and the Middle East, however, use much more for feed than other parts of the developing world, apparently because of differences in per capita incomes and preferences.

More significant for the agricultural exporting countries is that the use of basic food staples for feed is increasing faster than their use for food. The growth rate for cereal feed was between 4 and 5 percent for most of the LDCs and 4.6 percent overall. More than 90 percent of all feed consisted of cereals by the late 1970s. Thus the data suggest a high and growing use of cereals for feed throughout the LDCs. Given the high income elasticity of the demand for feed, this pattern reflects a potentially high growth of demand for cereals by LDCs wherever high income growth rates are achieved.

Table 9 presents food trade data for the LDCs. Although some regions had positive net trade balances for major food staples in the late 1960s, every region of the developing world except lower South America had a negative net figure by the late 1970s. Overall, the LDCs' imports of food staples grew about two and one-third times as fast as their exports, leading to a trade deficit approaching 40 million metric tons in the late 1970s. The growth in food imports largely reflects the growth in cereal imports for both human and animal consumption.

The Soviet Union and Eastern Europe have not experienced large changes in production or productivity in agriculture, especially in grain production. Total grain production in the Soviet Union has been erratic over the past twenty years, and there is little evidence of an upward trend. A growth in per capita income, however, has increased the demand for imports significantly. Grain imports have increased from very low levels in the late 1960s to between 30 and 50 million metric tons in the 1980s. The observed pattern of imports suggests that they have moved in response to variations in domestic production and to the availability of hard currency. The decline in energy prices in the 1980s and the associated decline in the availability of hard currency have corresponded to a decline in Soviet agricultural imports, especially of grains.[4]

Development Assistance and Agricultural Research

Official development assistance from all sources has grown dramatically since World War II. Almost nonexistent before the war, assistance totaled over $21 billion by 1970 in 1981 U.S. dollars and increased to over $36 billion by 1980 (table 10). About $1 billion of

41

TABLE 6
Changes in Production of Major Food Crops and Their Contributions to the Total Production Change, by Region, 1960–1985
(millions of metric tons)

Commodity	Developing Market Economies		Asia		Africa		Latin America	
	Increase	Share of total (percent)	Increase	Share of total (percent)	Increase	Share of total (percent)	Increase	Share of total (percent)
Major food crops								
1960–1965	48.0	100	24	100	7.5	100	16.5	100
1965–1970	43.5	100	37	100	–9	100	15.5	100
1970–1975	60	100	44.5	100	9	100	6.5	100
1975–1980	72	100	56	100	8	100	7.5	100
1980–1985	115	100	68	100	21.5	100	25.5	100
Cereal grains								
1960–1965	46.5	97	25	—	7	93	14.5	88
1965–1970	45	—	39.5	—	–9	100	14.5	94
1970–1975	45	75	35.5	80	0.5	6	9	—
1975–1980	55	76	46	82	2	25	7	93
1980–1985	86	75	53	78	9	42	24	94

Noncereals

1960–1965	1.5	3	−1	—	0.5	7	2	12
1965–1970	−1.5	—	−2.5	—	0	0	1	6
1970–1975	15	25	9	20	8.5	94	−2.5	—
1975–1980	17	24	10	18	6	75	0.5	7
1980–1985	29	25	15	22	12.5	58	1.5	6

Hectares of Arable Land and Permanent Crops
(millions)

	Developing market economies	Asia	Africa	Latin America
1960	671	342	226	103
1970	664	342	187	134
1980	674	351	151	172
1984	686	355	154	177

SOURCE: FAO, *FAO Production Yearbook*, vols. 15, 29, 30, 34, 39.

43

TABLE 7

Average Annual Growth Rates of Production, Area Harvested, and Output per Hectare of Major Food Crops, by Region and Subregion, 1961–1980

(percent)

	Average Annual Growth Rate			Contribution to Production Increase	
	Production	Area harvested	Output per hectare	Area harvested	Output per hectare
Developing countries	3.1	0.8	2.3	25	75
(Excluding China)	(2.6)	(1.0)	(1.6)	(38)	(62)
Asia	3.4	0.5	2.9	15	85
(Excluding China)	(2.8)	(0.7)	(2.1)	(26)	(74)
China	4.1	0.1	4.0	3	97
South Asia	2.7	0.6	2.0	23	77
East and Southeast Asia	3.1	1.1	2.0	35	65
North Africa and Middle East	2.5	1.0	1.5	40	60
Northern Africa	2.3	1.8	0.5	79	21
Western Asia	2.6	0.6	2.0	23	77
Sub-Saharan Africa	1.7	1.4	0.4	79	21
West Africa	0.8	1.1	−0.3	100	—
Central Africa	2.9	3.3	−0.4	100	—
Eastern and southern Africa	2.5	1.2	1.3	47	53
Latin America	2.8	1.5	1.3	52	48
Mexico and Central America	3.4	0.6	2.9	17	83
Upper South America	2.8	2.6	0.2	92	8
Lower South America	2.3	0.2	2.1	7	93

Source: Paulino, *Food in the Third World.*

assistance was allocated to agriculture and about $2.6 billion to food aid in 1982.

The countries of North America, Oceania, and Western Europe have consistently contributed nearly half the world's national spending on agricultural research. National research spending rose from $5.3 billion in 1970 to nearly $7.4 billion in 1980.

The Consultative Group on International Agricultural Research (CGIAR) was established in the mid-1960s. Its international agri-

TABLE 8: Consumption of Basic Food Staples, by Region and Subregion, 1966–1980
(percent)

	Average Annual Growth Rate of Consumption				Domestic Use, 1966–1970			Domestic Use, 1976–1980		
	Total	Food	Feed	Other	Food	Feed	Other	Food	Feed	Other
Developing countries	3.3	3.2	4.3	2.5	70	14	16	69	16	15
(Excluding China)	(3.0)	(2.8)	(4.3)	(2.4)	(67)	(16)	(17)	(65)	(18)	(17)
Asia	3.3	3.3	4.2	2.8	75	11	14	75	11	14
(Excluding China)	(3.0)	(2.9)	(4.1)	(2.7)	(74)	(10)	(16)	(73)	(11)	(16)
China	3.8	3.7	4.4	2.9	76	11	13	76	12	12
South Asia	2.7	2.7	2.8	2.8	75	9	16	74	9	17
East and Southeast Asia	3.5	3.2	5.7	2.6	73	12	15	72	15	13
North Africa and Middle East	3.9	3.7	4.8	3.2	56	24	20	55	26	19
Northern Africa	4.3	3.9	6.9	3.1	66	17	17	64	21	15
Western Asia	3.6	3.5	4.1	3.3	51	27	22	50	29	21
Sub-Saharan Africa	2.2	2.5	3.1	1.3	71	6	23	73	6	21
West Africa	2.3	2.7	3.6	1.1	66	5	29	69	5	26
Central Africa	2.7	2.7	3.7	2.8	82	4	14	81	4	15
Eastern and southern Africa	1.9	2.0	2.7	1.3	73	8	19	73	8	19
Latin America	3.1	2.4	4.4	2.0	50	34	16	47	39	14
Mexico and Central America	4.3	3.0	7.5	2.8	62	26	12	55	34	11
Upper South America	3.0	2.3	4.3	2.0	48	34	18	45	38	17
Lower South America	1.4	1.3	1.6	0.8	34	49	17	34	50	16

Source: Paulino, *Food in the Third World*.

45

TABLE 9

Exports, Imports, and Net Trade of Major Food Staples, by Region and Subregion, 1966–1970 and 1976–1980

	Exports			Imports			Net Trade (millions of metric tons)		Average Annual Growth Rate, 1966–70 to 1976–80 (percent)	
	1966–70 (millions of metric tons)	1976–80	Change (percent)	1966–70 (millions of metric tons)	1976–80	Change (percent)	1966–70	1976–80	Exports	Imports
Developing countries	28.83	37.47	30	40.99	75.36	84	−12.16	−37.89	2.7	6.3
(Excluding China)	(26.85)	(35.80)	(33)	(35.16)	(63.06)	(79)	(−8.31)	(−27.26)	(2.9)	(6.0)
Asia	9.61	15.98	66	23.78	32.24	36	−14.17	−16.26	5.2	3.1
(Excluding China)	(7.63)	(14.31)	(88)	(17.95)	(19.94)	(11)	(−10.32)	(−5.63)	(6.5)	(1.1)
China	1.98	1.67	−16	5.83	12.30	111	−3.85	−10.63	−1.7	7.8
South Asia	1.88	3.18	69	10.07	5.73	−43	−8.19	−2.55	5.4	−5.5
East and Southeast Asia	5.75	11.13	94	7.88	14.21	80	−2.13	−3.08	6.8	6.1

North Africa and Middle East	1.95	2.22	14	6.74	19.28	186	−4.79	−17.06	1.3	11.1
Northern Africa	1.37	0.82	−40	3.98	10.76	170	−2.61	−9.94	−5.0	10.5
Western Asia	0.58	1.40	142	2.76	8.52	209	−2.18	−7.13	9.2	11.9
Sub-Saharan Africa	3.89	1.86	−52	2.60	6.25	140	1.29	−4.39	−7.1	9.2
West Africa	2.51	1.08	−57	1.11	3.37	203	1.40	−2.29	−8.1	11.7
Central Africa	0.26	0.06	−78	0.39	0.87	124	−0.13	−0.82	−13.9	8.4
Eastern and southern Africa	1.13	0.72	−36	1.10	2.00	82	0.03	−1.28	−4.4	6.2
Latin America	13.38	17.41	30	7.87	17.59	123	5.51	−0.18	2.7	8.4
Mexico and Central America	1.71	0.87	−49	2.34	6.65	184	−0.63	−5.78	−6.6	11.0
Upper South America	1.99	1.79	−10	4.82	9.69	101	−2.83	−7.90	−1.0	7.2
Lower South America	9.68	14.76	52	0.71	1.25	76	8.97	13.50	4.3	5.8

SOURCE: Paulino, *Food in the Third World.*

47

TABLE 10

EXPENDITURES ON OFFICIAL DEVELOPMENT ASSISTANCE AND ON
AGRICULTURAL RESEARCH, 1970, 1980, AND 1982
(millions of 1981 dollars)

	1970	1980	1982
Official development assistance	21,300	36,210	34,970
Bilateral	18,450	28,650	27,370
Multilateral	2,860	7,560	7,610
Grants by private voluntary associations	2,220	2,240	2,360
Development commitments by purpose			
Total	—	—	32,070
Allocable by sector	—	—	16,680
Agriculture	—	—	1,000
Not allocable by sector	—	—	15,380
Food aid	—	—	2,640
National agricultural research	5,340	7,390	n.a.
North America, Oceania, Western Europe	2,400	3,210	n.a.
Soviet Union and Eastern Europe	1,280	1,490	n.a.
Developing countries	1,670	2,680	n.a.
CGIAR expenditures[a]	20	140	140

n.a. = not available.
a. Consultative Group on International Agricultural Research.
SOURCE: Jock Anderson, "International Agricultural Research Centers:
Achievements and Potential," draft prepared August 31, 1985, for the CGIAR.

cultural research centers (IARCs) grew with and fostered the "green revolution" brought about by the dissemination of semidwarf wheat and rice varieties developed by the first two IARCs, in Mexico and the Philippines. In 1970 there were four IARCs with total budgets of only $20 million; by 1980 there were fourteen with total budgets of $140 million.

The IARCs focus primarily on developing improved varieties of food crops and transferring them to developing countries. The centers have provided a means of transferring innovations based on crop germ plasm to national research organizations along with the knowledge of how those innovations can be adapted to local conditions. Most of the tangible economic benefits of the CGIAR research can be attributed to the modern wheat and rice varieties that have been widely adopted throughout the world, which are due in part to the genetic material developed at the IARCs.

Strong national research organizations are needed to derive the most benefits from existing research developments such as those produced by the IARCs. This need has been recognized by governments of the developing countries, which have made substantial investments in research capability. Recent decades have seen high rates of growth in the numbers of researchers employed, though not in all countries (table 11). Agricultural research and extension expenditures, as a percentage of agricultural product, have been growing steadily throughout the world (table 12). Low-income countries have roughly tripled their spending on research and extension during the 1960–1980 period.

As a result of these efforts, modern agricultural technology has spread remarkably in the LDCs. During the 1974–1984 period, for example, the use of fertilizers in the LDCs doubled from about 12 to 24 million metric tons per year.[5] Table 13 summarizes the use of major inputs in LDC agriculture in the 1969–1980 period. While the traditional inputs of land, human labor, and animal labor increased moderately, fertilizer use increased more than 150 percent and machinery use more than 125 percent. At the same time the modern semidwarf wheat and rice varieties spread throughout the world. The area under semidwarf wheat increased to almost 50 percent of the total acreage in wheat in 1983 from only 14 percent in 1970 while the area in semidwarf rice increased from 30 to nearly 60 percent (table 14).

Despite the frequently used term "green revolution" to describe the introduction of the new wheat and rice varieties, a careful look at the research leading to their development suggests that a better label might be "green evolution." The introduction of the new wheat varieties in the mid-1960s in India was a remarkable success, but many years of research in Mexico, by Normal Bourlag and others, was needed for that achievement in India. With the advent of the organized research activities centered at the IARCs, it seems unlikely that such a discrete advance in agricultural productivity will occur in the future. Smaller but continual incremental productivity gains are likely as varieties are improved and associated production practices and inputs are refined.

Important limitations remain to existing agricultural technology's potential for enhancing productivity in developing countries. First, the modern wheat and rice varieties perform well within a relatively narrow range of environmental conditions. Those conditions do not exist in many of the poor, food-deficit regions of the world. In regions endowed with a suitable natural environment, the modern varieties require adequate water, so that the availability of irrigation has become a major constraint in arid parts of the world. The potential yield of the modern varieties is obtained only with application of nitrogen fertilizer, so that farmers must have access to fertilizer as well as the

TABLE 11
STATUS AND GROWTH OF NATIONAL
AGRICULTURAL RESEARCH SYSTEMS, 1964–1984

| Country | Number of Agricultural Researchers Excluding University Staff, 1982 | | | Growth Rate of Number of Researchers | |
	With higher degrees[a]	Total[b]	Per million hectares	Percent	Years covered
Africa					
Cameroon		176	—	5	1965–84
Ethiopia	50	123	9	9	1972–82
Kenya	315	638	335	8	1970–82
Malawi	21	76	33	6	1964–83
Nigeria	276	491	18	17	1970–80
Senegal	n.a.	196	39	9	1975–84
Tanzania	n.a.	236	58	18	1970–82
Zimbabwe	n.a.	214	79	1	1970–84
Asia					
Bangladesh	1,262	1,514	170	n.a.	
Burma	30	266	27	n.a.	
India	547	5,977	35	n.a.	
Indonesia	400	1,360	95	24	1975–84
Nepal	170	388	169	11	1971–80
Philippines	105	1,330	171	n.a.	
Thailand	n.a.	8,356	489	6	1975–82
Latin America					
Brazil	1,275	1,613	25	n.a.	
Chile	62	171	32	1	1970–82
Colombia	228	426[c]	104	n.a.	
Costa Rica	7	70	233	n.a.	
Ecuador	75	337	187	n.a.	
Guatemala	30	210	161	n.a.	
Mexico	360	1,240	56	11	1970–82
Peru	32	250	78	3	1970–83
Middle East and North Africa					
Egypt	1,427	3,556	1,459	10	1979–81
Syria	55	500	95	n.a.	

n.a. = not available.
a. Master's and doctoral degrees.
b. Degree holder and above.
c. Research workers of International Institute for Agricultural Science.
SOURCE: Anderson, "International Agricultural Research Centers."

TABLE 12

Research and Extension Expenditures as a Percentage of the Value of Agricultural Product, Public Sector, 1959, 1970, and 1980

	Agricultural Research Expenditures			Agricultural Extension Expenditures		
	1959	1970	1980	1959	1970	1980
Northern Europe	0.55	1.05	1.60	0.65	0.85	0.84
Central Europe	0.39	1.20	1.54	0.29	0.42	0.45
Southern Europe	0.24	0.61	0.74	0.11	0.35	0.28
Eastern Europe	0.50	0.81	0.78	0.32	0.36	0.40
Soviet Union	0.43	0.73	0.70	0.28	0.32	0.35
Oceania	0.99	2.24	2.83	0.42	0.76	0.98
North America	0.84	1.27	1.09	0.42	0.53	0.56
Temperate South America	0.39	0.64	0.70	0.07	0.50	0.43
Tropical South America	0.25	0.67	0.98	0.34	0.71	1.19
Caribbean and Central America	0.15	0.22	0.63	0.09	0.18	0.33
North Africa	0.31	0.62	0.59	1.27	2.21	1.71
West Africa	0.37	0.61	1.19	0.58	1.24	1.28
East Africa	0.19	0.53	0.81	0.67	0.88	1.16
Southern Africa	1.13	1.10	1.23	1.64	0.67	0.46
West Asia	0.18	0.37	0.47	0.25	0.57	0.51
South Asia	0.12	0.19	0.43	0.20	0.23	0.20
Southeast Asia	0.10	0.28	0.52	0.24	0.37	0.36
East Asia	0.69	2.01	2.44	0.19	0.67	0.85
China	0.09	0.68	0.56	n.a.	n.a.	n.a.
Country group						
Low-income developing	0.15	0.27	0.50	0.30	0.43	0.44
Middle-income developing	0.29	0.57	0.81	0.60	1.01	0.92
Semi-industrialized	0.29	0.54	0.73	0.29	0.51	0.59
Industrialized	0.68	1.37	1.50	0.38	0.57	0.62
Planned	0.33	0.73	0.66	—	—	—
Planned, excluding China	0.45	0.75	0.73	0.29	0.33	0.36

n.a. = not available.

SOURCE: M. Ann Judd, James K. Boyce, and Robert E. Evenson, "Investing in Agricultural Supply," *Economic Development and Cultural Change*, vol. 35 (1986), pp. 77–114.

TABLE 13

Use of Major Inputs in Agricultural Production, Developing Countries, by Region, 1969–1971 and 1980

Region	Year	Land[a] (million hectares)	Labor[b] (millions)	Fertilizer (million tons)	Draft Animals[c] (millions)	Machinery[d] (thousands)
China	1969–71	102.2	268.3	4.3	93.1	144
	1980	99.2	276.5	12.8	95.5	766
India	1969–71	164.7	153.8	1.9	236.8	112
	1980	169.1	165.9	5.0	246.5	419
Other developing Asia[e]	1969–71	102.9	126.9	3.0	115.8	104
	1980	111.5	142.8	7.5	133.8	321
Middle East and North Africa	1969–71	84.6	31.8	1.1	60.7	208
	1980	87.3	34.9	3.0	72.7	645
Sub-Saharan Africa	1969–71	139.5	87.6	1.7	147.2	165
	1980	150.2	100.8	1.2	162.1	226
Latin America	1969–71	146.4	36.5	2.9	255.2	725
	1980	162.1	39.0	6.8	305.5	1,012
All developing countries	1969–71	741.5	706.2	13.3	909.3	1,463
	1980	780.6	759.4	34.2	1,016.7	3,305

a. Arable and permanent crop land.
b. Economically active population in agriculture. Note that national data generally do not include nonmarket agricultural labor of women and children and exclude or undercount part-time and periodic wage work of women in agriculture.
c. Horses, mules, asses, cattle, buffalo, and camels.
d. Number of agricultural tractors plus harvesters and threshers in use.
e. FAO's categories of Far East plus Asian centrally planned economies less India and China.
SOURCE: Anderson, "International Agricultural Research Centers."

financial ability to purchase it in adequate quantities at appropriate times during the growing season. Farmers are often located far from markets in which they could sell the surplus production that they might be able to obtain from the new varieties. Without such markets the incentive to increase production is greatly diminished.

A new development on the technological horizon, however, appears to have the potential to surpass the achievements of the green revolution and to overcome the limitations of the existing technology. That new development is the "biorevolution," the application of the new biogenetic techniques that are possible with recent advances in molecular and cell biology. Those techniques open the possibility of making progress in important areas where the existing agricultural

TABLE 14
AREAS UNDER SEMIDWARF WHEAT AND SEMIDWARF RICE, 1970 AND 1983

	Semidwarf Wheat, 1970		Semidwarf Rice, 1970		Semidwarf Wheat, 1983		Semidwarf Rice, 1983	
	Area (thousand hectares)	Percent	Area (thousand hectares)	Percent	Area (thousand hectares)	Percent	Area (thousand hectares)	Percent
China	14.7	0.1	26,848.0	77.3	5,126.0	17.8	32,265.2	95.0
India	6,480.0	39.0	5,588.0	14.8	18,550.0	80.1	22,180.0	54.1
Other developing Asia	3,458.6	40.1	4,281.5	10.0	7,797.1	68.8	19,734.1	42.4
Sub-Saharan Africa	69.8	5.0	40.9	4.1	556.3	52.1	241.9	14.8
Latin America	794.5	10.8	252.4	4.2	8,878.0	82.5	1,831.7	27.8
Middle East and North Africa	1,144.4	5.0	2.1	0.3	7,690.3	33.8	80.7	11.0
All developing countries	11,962.0	14.0	37,012.9	30.1	48,597.7	49.7	76,333.6	58.5

SOURCE: Anderson, "International Agricultural Research Centers."

technology has run into severe obstacles. In the areas of tolerance to drought and salinity, nitrogen fixation, pest resistance, and efficiency of water use, the biogenetic techniques may be able to make substantial advances where conventional plant breeding has thus far failed.

Perhaps the most profound change biogenetics might have on agricultural development is in the scope of new agricultural innovations. According to one study of the new technologies, "The biorevolution will permit the extension of commercial agriculture to all regions, including those characterized by marginal soils . . . the impact of the biorevolution has the potential to encompass the entire rural population."[6] In contrast to the green revolution, which was limited to plant improvement, the biorevolution will probably increase productivity in both plants and animals. One of the most promising developments in biogenetic work so far, for example, is the development of a bovine growth hormone, whose introduction might increase dairy production 20 to 30 percent.[7]

If such remarkable developments are indeed forthcoming, they might rapidly ameliorate the food problems of LDCs. These promising biogenetic advances remain speculative, however. It is entirely possible that, like the modern plant breeding work before them, they will encounter unanticipated difficulties that limit their potential. How far biogenetics will contribute to food production remains to be demonstrated.

Notes

1. National Academy of Sciences, *The Growth of World Population* (Washington, D.C.: National Academy Press, 1963).

2. Note that total production, A, can be written as $A = (A/H)(H)$, that is, as yield, A/H, times acreage, H. Converting this expression to growth rates, one obtains $a = y + h$, where a is the growth rate in output, y is the growth rate in yield, and h is the growth rate in acreage.

3. See Leonardo A. Paulino, *Food in the Third World: Past Trends and Projections to 2000* (Washington, D.C.: International Food Policy Research Institute, 1986), table 24.

4. U.S. Department of Agriculture, *USSR, Situation and Outlook Report* (Economic Research Service, May 1986).

5. U.S. Department of Agriculture, *World Agriculture, Outlook and Situation Report* (Economic Research Service, September 1985).

6. Frederick H. Buttel, Martin Kenney, and Jack Kloppenburg, "From Green Revolution to Biorevolution: Some Observations on the Changing Technological Bases of Economic Transformation in the Third World," *Economic Development and Cultural Change,* vol. 34 (1985), pp. 31–55.

7. See Office of Technology Assessment, *Technology, Public Policy, and the Changing Structure of American Agriculture: Summary* (Washington, D.C.: U.S. Congress, March 1986).

5
World Agricultural Development: Projections to 2000

This chapter summarizes recent attempts to predict trends in such key variables as population, income, and production into the twenty-first century. The chapter begins with projections of global population and economic growth and proceeds to projections of economic growth and agricultural production growth in the developed countries and of production, demand, and trade in the less-developed countries.

These projections have been obtained by various quantitative methods. The simplest are based on extrapolations of past trends, others on complex models, and still others on both models and expert judgment. Simple extrapolations of past trends are often good predictors in the very short term but become less reliable in the longer term. The projections presented here have been drawn from sources reflecting some of the best expertise in the field and can thus be considered as reliable as any existing estimates.[1]

Global Population and Economic Growth

World population projections based on various models and methods are presented in table 15. The 1980 population of about 4.5 billion will have increased one-third to one-half by the year 2000 or soon thereafter. The most conservative projections foresee a population of 5.8 billion for the year 2000, and some are as high as 6.5 billion. Projections to 2020 estimate a population of 7 to 8 billion. Regardless of the particular projection one chooses to believe, it is clear that unless population growth rates in the LDCs decrease rapidly in the near future, there will be nearly 6 billion people on the planet by the year 2000. Regional population projections are presented in table 16.

Table 17 presents projected growth rates of real output by region. For much of the world output growth rates of 2–3 percent per capita are expected. East Asia is projected to grow at a much higher 4 percent and sub-Saharan Africa to experience a decline due to a

TABLE 15: SHORT- AND LONG-TERM WORLD POPULATION PROJECTIONS

Model or Source	Kind of Projection	Population in 2000 (billions)	Longer-Term Projections
World 3	Standard run	6.0	Population increases to 7.0 billion by 2025, then decreases to 4.0 billion by 2100
	Equilibrium run	NA	Population stabilizes at 6.0 billion by 2050
World integrated model	Standard run	6.4	Population stabilizes at just under 7.0 billion by 2015; death rates due to starvation high in South Asia
Latin American world model	Standard run	6.4	Population reaches 11.0 billion by 2040 and is still growing at 1.1 percent per year; death rates due to starvation rising rapidly in Asia
	Second run (improved conditions in Asia)	NA	Population reaches almost 11.0 billion by 2060 and is growing at less than 0.5 percent per year
United Nations	1978 assessment (provisional)	5.9 to 6.5	Population reaches 8.0 to 12.0 billion by 2050 and stabilizes at 8.0 to 14.0 billion by 2150
Global 2000 (Census Bureau)	High, medium, low	5.8 to 6.5	NA
CFSC	High, medium, low	5.8 to 6.0	Population reaches 7.8 to 8.1 billion by 2050 and is virtually stationary
World Bank	Standard	6.0	Population stabilizes at 9.8 billion by 2175
Harvard	Standard	5.9	Population reaches 8.4 billion by 2075 and is virtually stationary

NA = not applicable.
SOURCE: Office of Technology Assessment, *Global Models, World Futures, and Public Policy* (Washington, D.C., 1982).

TABLE 16

HISTORICAL AND PROJECTED POPULATION, ABSOLUTE CHANGE, AND GROWTH RATES, BY REGION, 1980–2000
(millions)

	1980 Population	1980–1990 Absolute change	1980–1990 Rate of growth (%)	1990–1995 Absolute change	1990–1995 Rate of growth (%)	1995–2000 Absolute change	1995–2000 Rate of growth (%)	2000 Population
North Africa and Middle East	243	70	2.56	35	2.12	40	2.22	388
Sub-Saharan Africa	387	141	3.16	95	3.37	105	3.15	727
European Community	270	7	0.26	5	0.34	4	0.30	286
Other Western Europe	79	5	0.62	2	0.54	2	0.46	88
Soviet Union	265	26	0.94	11	0.73	10	0.63	312
Eastern Europe	135	9	0.65	4	0.56	4	0.54	152
South Asia	874	216	2.24	112	1.97	112	1.80	1,315
East Asia	459	87	1.75	45	1.59	45	1.47	635
Asia, centrally planned economies	1,075	161	1.41	82	1.30	80	1.18	1,398
Oceania	23	3	1.23	1	1.10	1	0.99	28
Latin America	359	90	2.26	48	2.03	47	1.83	544
North America	252	20	0.73	8	0.60	7	0.50	287
World total	4,421	835	1.75	448	1.65	457	1.55	6,160

SOURCE: Resources for the Future, *Global Demand for U.S. Food and Fiber.*

TABLE 17
Historical and Projected Total and Per Capita Economic Growth Rates, 1985–2000
(percent)

	1985 Total	1985 Per capita	1990 Total	1990 Per capita	1995 Total	1995 Per capita	2000 Total	2000 Per capita
North Africa and Middle East	4.17	1.5	3.99	1.5	3.62	1.5	3.72	1.5
Sub-Saharan Africa	2.57	−0.5	2.72	−0.5	3.37	0	3.15	0
European Economic Community	2.41	2.2	2.50	2.2	2.54	2.2	2.50	2.2
Other Western Europe	3.57	2.5	3.07	2.5	3.04	2.5	2.96	2.5
Soviet Union	3.49	2.5	3.38	2.5	3.23	2.5	3.13	2.5
Eastern Europe	3.21	2.5	3.11	2.5	3.16	2.5	3.04	2.5
South Asia	3.83	1.5	3.64	1.5	3.47	1.5	3.30	1.5
East Asia	5.81	4.0	5.70	4.0	4.59	3.0	4.47	3.0
Asia, centrally planned economies	4.32	2.9	4.80	2.9	4.20	2.9	4.08	2.9
Oceania	3.71	2.5	3.68	2.5	3.60	2.5	3.49	2.5
Latin America	4.64	2.3	4.50	2.3	4.33	2.3	4.13	2.3
North America	3.50	2.7	3.43	2.7	3.30	2.7	3.20	2.7

Source: Resources for the Future, *Global Demand for U.S. Food and Fiber.*

relatively low rate of growth in production and the highest population growth rate in the world.

Table 18 presents projections of population, growth of GDP, and cereal demand and supply for the year 2000 that illustrate the extent to which the various world models yield different projections. For example, the IIASA and AT-2000 models predict aggregate average growth rates for the developing countries higher than 3 percent per year while the GOL model (the grain, oils, and livestock model of the U.S. Department of Agriculture) predicts less than 2 percent. Cereal demand and supply likewise show considerable discrepancies among models. Yet all the models yield the same qualitative result regarding net exports of grains: the developed market economies will be large net exporters, and the developing countries will be large net importers. Of course, this is not surprising given the historical evolution of cereal trade discussed in chapter 4. Except for the Global 2000, however, the models predict that by 2000 imports by the developing countries will have more than doubled the 1980 figure of about 46 million metric tons.

These large models also generate projections of the prices of

TABLE 18

GLOBAL MODELS' PROJECTIONS OF WORLD POPULATION, ECONOMIC GROWTH, AND CEREAL DEMAND AND SUPPLY TO THE YEAR 2000

	World	Developed Market Economies	Planned Economies	Developing Countries
Change in population (%)				
AT-2000	1.7	0.6	1.0	2.4
Global 2000	1.8	0.5	1.2	2.4
GOL 1984	1.7	0.6	1.2	2.3
IIASA				
1980–1990	1.8	0.8	0.8[a]	2.5
1990–2000	1.7	0.7	0.7	2.4
EPI/RFF	1.8	0.5[b]	1.2	2.2[c]
World Bank	1.6	0.6	1.0	2.3
Change in GDP (%)				
AT-2000				
1980–1990	n.a.	2.4	2.5[a]	3.2
1990–2000	n.a.	2.5	2.5	3.4
Global 2000	1.5	2.6	2.2	2.0
GOL 1984	1.3	2.1	1.8	1.8
IIASA				
1980–1990	2.5	2.8	4.5[a]	3.1
1990–2000	2.3	2.4	4.2	3.2
EPI/RFF	1.7	2.5[b]	2.1	2.3[c]
Change in cereal demand (%)				
AT-2000	1.8	1.2	1.3[a]	3.0
Global 2000	3.0	2.8	2.4	4.1
GOL 1984	1.9	1.4	1.6	2.7
IIASA	n.a.	1.4	1.2	3.1
EPI/RFF	1.9	1.2	1.7	2.8
Cereal demand in 2000 (millions of metric tons)				
AT-2000	n.a.	563	407[a]	768
Global 2000	2,197	648	759	790
GOL 1984	2,399	715	822	862
IIASA	2,029	612	636	781
EPI/RFF	2,119	522	836	767
Cereal production in 2000 (millions of metric tons)				
AT-2000	1,819[a]	730	449[a]	640
Global 2000	2,197	740	722	735
GOL 1984	2,398	937	733	728

(Table continues)

TABLE 18 (continued)

	World	Developed Market Economies	Planned Economies	Developing Countries
IIASA	2,027	779	593	656
EPI/RFF	2,118	709	754	656
Net exports in 2000 (millions of metric tons)				
AT-2000	0	209	−10[a]	−117
Global 2000	0	91	−37	−55
GOL 1984	0	222	−89	−134
IIASA	0	167	−43	−125
EPI/RFF	0	187	−82	−106

NOTE: Models are as follows: AT-2000, *Agriculture toward 2000*, Food and Agriculture Organization, 1981; Global 2000, *The Global Report to the President*, Council on Environmental Quality, 1980; GOL 1984, Grain-Oil-Livestock Model Projections, Department of Agriculture, 1984; IIASA, International Institute for Applied Systems Analysis, 1984; EPI/RFF, Economic Perspectives, Inc./Resources for the Future, 1983. Base years are as follows: AT-2000, 1978–1979; Global 2000, 1973–1975; GOL 1984, 1980; IIASA, 1980; EPI/RFF, 1978–1979 to 1980–1981. n.a. = not available.
a. Excludes China.
b. Excludes Japan.
c. Includes Japan.
SOURCE: Rachael Sarko, "Agricultural Trade Model Comparisons: A Look at Agricultural Markets in the Year 2000," Resources for the Future, Renewable Resources Discussion Paper no. 87-01, November 1986.

major agricultural commodities, some of which are presented in table 19. Although the Global 2000 model predicts rather large price increases (apparently because of its pessimistic assumptions about growing population and resource scarcity), the IIASA and GOL models imply much more moderate price changes over the 1980–2000 period.[2] Since market price is a function of world supply and demand, the outcome depends on whether demand grows more rapidly than supply. For commodities such as wheat, where national policies have a major effect on the world price, it is also a function of those policies.[3]

Projections for the United States and Other Developed Countries

Projections of world demand for U.S. agricultural products and of U.S. production of grains and oilseeds are presented in tables 20 and

21, and figure 8 shows the gradual rise in U.S. agricultural exports during the 1950–1970 period, with the dramatic upturn in the 1970s. The subsequent reversal of the upward trend in the early 1980s has raised questions about U.S. ability to compete with other exporters. The reasons for the downturn have been hotly debated. Explanations have included growing world competition, U.S. macroeconomic policy, and U.S. embargoes and other agricultural policies.[4] The projections to the year 2000 in the figure are a linear trend representing a weighted average of the two trends of the 1950–1970 and 1970–1980 periods. An important question is whether the downturn in the early 1980s is merely temporary or reflects fundamental changes in the structure of international agricultural commodity markets.

U.S. domestic demand for major agricultural commodities seems unlikely to grow rapidly, because of the high U.S. income per capita and the low income elasticity for those commodities. The major source of demand growth must be international markets. This of course raises the question of the likely growth in production and demand in the rest of the world. Table 20 and figure 8 embody the assumption that growth in production throughout the world will be significant but not sufficiently great in relation to the growth in demand to cause a permanent decline in U.S. agricultural exports.

TABLE 19

PROJECTED WORLD AGRICULTURAL COMMODITY PRICE CHANGES TO THE YEAR 2000

(percent price change 1980–2000 unless otherwise noted)

Model	Scenario	Cereals	Livestock	Aggregate
Global 2000[a]	Alternative I			45 to 95
	Alternative II			30
	Alternative III			115
IIASA	Reference	−5 to 0	−1 to 16	−5
GOL 1984[b]	High income/policies	19	20	
	Base line	−3	−5	
	Low income/policies	−19	−17	
	Trend continuation	−1	7	

NOTE: For models, see table 18.
a. Measured index of real world prices from 1969–1971 to 2000. Alternative I is base line, II is combination of optimistic income growth and weather, and III is pessimistic with respect to income growth, weather, and energy prices.
b. High income/policies scenario assumes a 10 percent greater income and 35 percent higher trade ceilings in 2000 than the base line; low income/policies is the converse.
SOURCE: See table 18.

TABLE 20

HISTORICAL AND PROJECTED GLOBAL DEMAND FOR U.S. AGRICULTURAL PRODUCTS, 1969–1971 TO 2000
(millions of metric tons)

| | 1969–1971 | | | 1979–1981 | | | 2000 | | | Annual Growth of Total Demand (percent) | |
Commodity	Domestic	Net trade	Total	Domestic	Net trade	Total	Domestic	Net trade	Total	1969–71 to 1979–81	1979–81 to 2000
Cereals[a]	171.0	39.0	210.0	192.7	109.6	302.3	227.0	168.2	395.3	3.7	1.3
Oilseeds[b]	20.2	17.0	37.2	31.5	33.3	64.8	38.1	53.9	92.0	5.7	1.6
Meat	21.9	−0.6	21.3	24.5	0	24.5	29.2	0.1	29.3	1.4	0.9
Milk	53.4	−0.2	53.2	59.0	−0.8	58.2	71.1	−0.9	70.2	0.9	0.9
Cotton	1.71	0.51	2.22	1.47	1.54	3.01	1.42	2.20	3.62	3.1	0.9

a. Includes food, feed, seed, industrial use, and waste.
b. Includes oilseed trade, in oilseed equivalent.
SOURCE: Resources for the Future, *Global Demand for U.S. Food and Fiber.*

TABLE 21

HISTORICAL AND PROJECTED AREA AND YIELDS OF GRAINS AND OILSEEDS, UNITED STATES, 1969–1971 TO 2000

Commodity	Area (millions of hectares)			Yield (kilograms per hectare)			Production (millions of metric tons)		
	1969–71	1979–81	2000	1969–71	1979–81	2000	1969–71	1979–81	2000
Cereals	60.7	72.6	76.8	3,458	4,162	5,148	210.0	302.3	395.3
Wheat	18.7	28.9	29.0	2,144	2,291	2,375	40.0	66.2	68.8
Corn	23.7	29.7	36.5	5,164	6,500	7,900	122.6	192.9	288.7
Oilseeds	23.3	35.8	41.2	1,596	1,800	2,234	37.2	64.6	92.0
Soybeans	17.0	27.7	31.6	1,830	2,000	2,439	31.2	55.3	77.1
Cotton lint	4.54	5.38	5.75	490	560	630	2.22	3.00	3.62
Total area in cereals, oilseeds, and cotton	88.5	113.8	123.8						

SOURCE: Resources for the Future, *Global Demand for U.S. Food and Fiber.*

FIGURE 8

U.S. Agricultural Export Volume, 1950–1983,
and Projections to the Year 2000
(millions of metric tons)

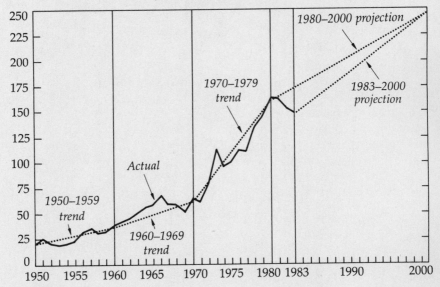

Source: Resources for the Future, *Global Demand for U.S. Food and Fiber.*

Table 22 presents one model's projection of cereal production for the various producing regions of the world. Note that Soviet production grew at only 0.33 percent during the 1970s but is projected to grow at 2.31 percent for the period 1979–1981 to 2000. Clearly, if the Soviet Union's growth rate is closer to its past performance, the trade prospects for the United States and other major grain exporters may be very different. Similarly, if China's economic performance and trade policies were altered, world market conditions might be very different from those portrayed in these projections.

Projections for the Developing Countries

Projections of production and consumption of major food crops in LDC regions and subregions are presented in table 23. The LDCs had a net deficit in their food production in 1980 of about 52 million metric tons, which is projected to grow to 69 million metric tons by the year 2000 and somewhat higher if China is not included. An important projected change is that Asia becomes a net exporter of over 50 million metric tons, roughly the amount of the LDC deficit in 1980. At the same time Africa's net deficit is projected to increase quite markedly and Latin America's to remain substantially the same.

Conclusions

The consensus of the various attempts to model and project major variables affecting agricultural development, such as population, income, food production, and trade, is of continued global growth and an increase in the volume of international trade in agricultural commodities. The developed market economies will export more food to the developing countries, but the extent of this trend will be diminished by the continuation of rapid production growth in Asia. A major factor driving the continued growth of exports from the more- to the less-developed countries will be the deterioration of production per capita in Africa.

These predictions must be interpreted carefully, however, be-

TABLE 22

PROJECTED RATES OF GROWTH OF CEREAL GRAIN PRODUCTION, BY REGION, 1969–1971 TO 2000

(percent)

	Area		Yield		Production	
	1969–71 to 1979–81	1979–81 to 2000	1969–71 to 1979–81	1979–81 to 2000	1969–71 to 1979–81	1979–81 to 2000
North Africa and Middle East	0.06	0.18	2.04	2.17	2.10	2.35
Sub-Saharan Africa	1.17	0.70	0.93	1.00	2.10	1.70
European Community	−0.09	−0.14	2.39	1.26	2.30	1.12
Other Western Europe	−0.17	−0.10	1.76	2.56	1.58	2.46
Soviet Union	0.53	0.05	−0.20	2.26	0.33	2.31
Eastern Europe	−0.43	0.08	2.75	1.08	2.31	1.16
South Asia	0.42	0.14	1.94	1.97	2.37	2.11
East Asia	1.12	1.28	1.47	1.21	2.60	2.51
Asia, centrally planned economies	0.21	−0.22	3.44	1.85	3.65	1.63
Oceania	3.20	2.10	0.78	1.16	4.00	3.29
Latin America	0.73	0.49	2.18	1.98	2.92	2.48
North America	1.75	0.24	1.71	1.11	3.50	1.35
World total	0.65	0.27	1.94	1.56	2.60	1.83

SOURCE: Resources for the Future, *Global Demand for U.S. Food and Fiber.*

TABLE 23
PRODUCTION AND CONSUMPTION OF MAJOR FOOD CROPS, BY REGION AND SUBREGION, 1980, AND PROJECTIONS TO 2000
(millions of metric tons)

| | 1980 | | | Projections to 2000 | | | | |
| | | | | At 1980 per capita consumption | | | With trend income growth | |
	Production	Consumption	Net surplus or deficit	Production	Consumption	Net surplus or deficit	Consumption	Net surplus or deficit
Developing countries	841.9	893.7	−51.8	1,471	1,315	156	1,540	−69
(Excluding China)	(543.1)	(579.8)	(−36.8)	(970)	(910)	(60)	(1,046)	(−76)
Asia	593.8	612.7	−18.9	1,035	847	187	983	51
(Excluding China)	(295.0)	(298.8)	(−3.8)	(534)	(442)	(91)	(489)	(44)
China	298.9	313.9	−15.0	501	405	96	494	7
South Asia	184.8	188.0	−3.3	323	282	41	310	13
East and Southeast Asia	110.2	110.8	−0.5	211	160	51	180	31

Region							
North Africa and Middle East	68.0	86.9	−18.9	119	145	−26	183	−64
Northern Africa	21.1	31.7	−10.6	35	55	−20	68	−33
Western Asia	46.9	55.2	−8.3	83	90	−7	114	−31
Sub-Saharan Africa	72.4	78.3	−5.9	114	149	−35	160	−47
West Africa	32.7	37.3	−4.7	39	69	−30	76	−36
Central Africa	12.1	13.0	−0.9	25	24	1	25	0
Eastern and southern Africa	27.6	27.9	−0.3	49	56	−7	60	−10
Latin America	107.7	115.9	−8.2	204	174	30	214	−9
Mexico and Central America	29.7	34.1	−4.4	57	55	2	65	−7
Upper South America	55.6	67.0	−11.5	100	97	3	126	−26
Lower South America	22.4	14.8	7.7	47	22	25	22	24

SOURCE: Paulino, *Food in the Third World*.

cause their reliability is difficult to assess. They are based largely on past trends; and "off-trend" events, such as the crop failure in the early 1970s in the Soviet Union, may significantly alter the course of events.[5] Moreover, small changes in assumptions and procedures can alter the results. One important component of the analysis of the growth of demand for cereals is the growth of demand for feed. Alternative methods of estimating demand for feed grains resulted in a projected demand 40 million metric tons higher in the IFPRI study, for example.[6] Such differences in assumptions presumably explain the large differences in the projections based on the various world models. Those in table 23, for example, when compared with those in table 18, appear to be more conservative than most of the other models except for Global 2000. These estimates suggest a large degree of uncertainty surrounding the predictions to the year 2000. The large differences in the projections—up to 80 million metric tons—would result in considerably different world market conditions, given that the U.S. export volume in the early 1980s was about 150 million metric tons.

Notes

1. This chapter draws on a variety of data sources, especially U.S. Congress, Office of Technology Assessment, *Global Models, World Futures, and Public Policy* (Washington, D.C., April 1982); Resources for the Future with Economic Perspectives, Inc., *Global Demand for U.S. Food and Fiber* (Washington, D.C.: Resources for the Future, 1983); and Leonardo A. Paulino, *Food in the Third World: Past Trends and Projections to 2000* (Washington, D.C.: International Food Policy Research Institute, 1986).

2. For detailed discussion of these models, see Rachel Sarko, "Agricultural Trade Model Comparisons: A Look at Agricultural Markets in the Year 2000," Resources for the Future, Renewable Resources Discussion Paper no. 87–01, November 1986.

3. The 1973 grain sales by the United States to the Soviet Union are a good example of how national policies can affect the world market.

4. See Bruce L. Gardner, ed., *U.S. Agricultural Policy: The 1985 Farm Legislation* (Washington, D.C.: American Enterprise Institute, 1985); and U.S. Department of Agriculture, Economic Research Service, *Embargoes, Surplus Disposal, and U.S. Agriculture*, Agricultural Economics Report no. 564, December 1986.

5. To illustrate the possibility of error in projections, even in sophisticated modeling exercises and for relatively short periods, consider that a 1973 study of the world wheat market predicted exports of wheat by the United States at 40 to 80 percent of the actual amount. Wheat imports by the developing countries were correspondingly underestimated by several studies. See Andrew Schmitz and D. Lee Bawden, *The World Wheat Economy: An Empirical*

Analysis, Monograph no. 32 (Berkeley: Giannini Foundation of Agricultural Economics, University of California, 1973); and Derek Byerlee, "The Political Economy of Third World Food Imports: The Case of Wheat," *Economic Development and Cultural Change*, vol. 35 (1987), pp. 307–28.

6. See Paulino, *Food in the Third World*, pp. 61–63.

6
The Future of U.S. Agriculture

This chapter synthesizes the qualitative analysis of the two-sector growth model of chapter 3 and the quantitative data of chapters 4 and 5 into models of the global agricultural economy, a price-taking open economy, and a price-making open economy. These stylized models are used to analyze the behavior of the world agricultural economy along its long-run trend. The rest of the chapter, building on the implications of these models, discusses topics related to the future of U.S. agriculture, including prospects for future growth and development around the world; the relevance of the "Asian model"; the role of technical assistance and foreign competition; equilibrium in U.S. agriculture; and the role of U.S. agricultural policy. The chapter concludes with a summary of the study's findings.

World Agricultural Development: Synthesis

Tables 24, 25, and 26 summarize some of the major theoretical implications of the growth model analysis of chapter 3 for the world, for a "small" price-taking open economy, and for a "large" price-making open economy. The small open economy represents small developing countries; the large open economy represents large developed countries like the United States and the European Community (EC) (the EC can be viewed as one economic unit for analytical purposes). The assumptions of the two-sector growth model are maintained, input-neutral and output-neutral technical change is assumed, and the income elasticity of demand for agricultural products is assumed to be less than unity.

Table 24 summarizes the qualitative effects of technical change and population growth on production levels and shares of the two sectors of the economy, labor employment in agriculture, and world product prices. Each exogenous effect (either technical change or population growth) is analyzed with the other held constant. A positive rate of population growth, with technical change held constant, generates a decline in per capita income and a shift in the demand function toward agriculture; a negative population growth

TABLE 24
Summary of World Model Results

	A		M		L		P_M/P_A
	Level	Share	Level	Share	Level	Share	
Technical change	+	−	+	+	−	−	+
Per capita income growth	−	−	+	+	−	−	+

NOTE: A = agricultural production; M = manufacturing production; L = labor in agriculture; P_M/P_A = ratio of manufacturing to agricultural prices.

rate has the opposite effect. Technical change and an increase in per capita income have similar effects on the world economy, except that technical change causes an increase in agricultural output whereas an increase in per capita income shifts the demand function toward nonagricultural products and thus leads to both a relative and an absolute decrease in agricultural production.

Overall, therefore, if we expect both technical change and per capita income growth to occur worldwide, we would expect to see a continued relative decline in agricultural output, both relative and absolute declines in agricultural employment, and a decline in the price of agricultural commodities. As we saw in chapter 4, this is indeed what has happened to the long-run trends in recent decades. From this set of assumptions we cannot conclude that agricultural output will necessarily increase; it is apparent, however, that during the past two decades the positive effect of technical change on production has dominated the negative demand-induced effects of per capita income growth, and agricultural output has in fact increased.

Table 25 summarizes the likely effects of exogenous variables on the production, consumption, and trade of a small open economy. The exogenous variables include technical change, growth in per capita income, agricultural price policy (in the form of price supports or output taxes), and changes in relative product prices.

In contrast to the closed economy, in which production must equal consumption, the production and consumption patterns of the small open economy need not be equal because it can trade its excess supply of one commodity to satisfy its excess demand for the other. Its production is driven by resource endowments, technology, and international prices; its consumption is determined by preferences, income, and international prices. Consequently, the effects of technical change and population growth in a small open economy are quite different from the effects on the global economy. Neutral technical change and population change leave the relative contribution of

71

TABLE 25
Summary of the Small Open Economy Model

| | Production | | | | | | Consumption | | Trade | |
| | A | | M | | L | | | | | |
	Level	Share	Level	Share	Level	Share	A	M	A exporter	M exporter
Technical change	+	0	+	0	0	0	+	+	?	?
Per capita income growth										
Positive	0	0	0	0	0	0	−	+	+	−
Negative	0	0	0	0	0	0	+	−	−	+
Agricultural price policy										
Support	+	+	−	−	+	+	−	−	+	?
Tax	−	−	+	+	−	−	−	−	?	+
Relative price (P_M/P_A) increase										
A exporter	−	−	+	+	+	+	−	+	?	
M exporter	+	+	−	−	+	+	+	+		?

NOTE: See note to table 24.

TABLE 26
SUMMARY OF THE LARGE OPEN ECONOMY MODEL

	Production						Consumption		Trade	
	A		M		L		A	M	A exporter	M exporter
	Level	Share	Level	Share	Level	Share				
Technical change										
A exporter										
Positive	+	0	+	0	0	0	+	+	?	?
Negative	−	−	+	+	−	−	−	+	?	?
M exporter										
Positive	−	−	+	+	−	−	?	+	?	?
Negative	+	+	−	−	+	+	?	−	?	?
Agricultural price policy										
A exporter										
Support	+	+	−	+	+	+	+	+	?	?
Tax	−	−	+	−	−	−	−	−	?	?
Relative price increase										
A exporter	−	−	−	+	−	−	−	−	?	?
M exporter	−	−	+	+	−	−	+	+		?

NOTE: See note to table 24.

agriculture to aggregate income unchanged. Technical change leads to higher consumption of both agricultural *(A)* and manufacturing *(M)* production, which, combined with the increases in production, makes it unclear whether the net effect on the country's trade volume will be an increase or a decrease.

The effects of population growth on trade are clearer. Because the income elasticity of demand for agricultural products is assumed to be less than unity, population growth that leads to a decline in per capita income shifts the demand function toward *A* and thus decreases exports if the country is an *A* exporter and increases exports if it is an *M* exporter. Exactly the opposite pattern holds if per capita income increases.

The effects of agricultural price policy on the small open economy are to distort production away from the pattern implied by comparative advantage and to reduce aggregate welfare through reduced consumption of both *M* and *A*, with corresponding changes in the volume of trade. Changes in world relative product prices also alter the country's production and consumption patterns with effects on trade. A rise in the price of *M* relative to that of *A* is bad for an agricultural exporter, causing a decline in aggregate consumption; the opposite is true for an *M* exporter. Predictions about the volume of trade cannot be made since production and consumption move in the same directions.

Table 26 summarizes results for the large open economy. The effects of technical change on production are identical with those of the world model. Since production and consumption of both goods increase, it is not possible to predict whether trade will increase or decrease.

Population growth and changes in per capita income have production effects similar to those of the world model, but the effects on consumption vary with the trade status of the economy. An *A* exporter with a decrease in population and a corresponding increase in per capita income, for example, decreases consumption of *A*. Since the demand shift toward *M* causes an increase in P_M/P_A, the consumption of *M* may increase or decrease; thus the changes in trade volume cannot be predicted.

Price policy for the large country can be thought of in terms of a monopoly or monopsony situation. The agricultural exporting country, for example, can invoke a price support program by restricting production domestically and driving up the world price. In principle such a policy can increase the country's welfare by improving its terms of trade vis-à-vis the rest of the world. The effect on trade is unclear, however, since both production and consumption of A decline. Similar results hold for the other cases considered in the table.

In summary, the theoretical models have definite qualitative implications for production and consumption patterns but ambiguous results for trade, especially for the large open economy model. The models fail to produce definite results for trade because production and consumption patterns tend to move together. To obtain a more definite picture of the likely patterns of trade for the small and large open economies, it is useful to appeal to the factual data. The data of chapter 4 showed that the developed countries are net agricultural exporters and the less-developed countries have become overwhelmingly net agricultural importers.

We can explain these facts by the influences of technical change, population growth, and agricultural policy. Technical change brought about an absolute growth in agricultural production in virtually all parts of the world but a global relative decline. Per capita income growth encouraged the relative decline of agricultural production, especially of low-income-elasticity staples. Some LDCs' policies also discouraged agricultural production. The trend in relative product prices moved against certain agricultural commodities produced by LDCs, such as rubber and sugar. The net effects of these factors were to encourage the relative decline of agricultural production and to reduce its absolute growth in LDCs below what it might otherwise have been. With per capita income growth came increased demand for relatively high-income-elasticity foods, especially cereals and meats.

Another major factor in the rise of developing countries' agricultural imports was a growth in the demand for feed grains. Feed grains are like a nonagricultural commodity in the analysis of the two-sector growth model because of their high income elasticity of demand. The factors that shift demand away from traditional agricultural products also raise the demand for feed grain imports.

In the developed countries, subsidies to and protection of agriculture encouraged production while demand growth was limited by the low income elasticities for basic agricultural commodities. With high rates of technological change, the absolute volume of output increased greatly, and agricultural producers searched for foreign markets for that output. At the same time crop failures in the Soviet Union in the early 1970s and the entry of the Soviets into the international grain market offered greater opportunities for export by the United States and other surplus countries. The high support prices of the United States in the early 1980s continued to give producers around the world incentives to increase production for export despite record world grain crops. The combined effect of these events was to create more integrated international commodity markets than had existed a decade earlier.

Prospects for Future Growth and Development

The projections of agricultural production, demand, and trade presented in chapter 5 suggest that the "stylized facts" describing the past several decades are likely to continue to represent the pattern of world agricultural development along the trend path for the foreseeable future. The developed countries are likely to continue to export large quantities of agricultural products, especially cereals, to the less-developed countries. The volume of agricultural commodities traded in international agricultural markets should increase.

Economic growth and development have been continuing in most third world countries since the 1950s: in low-income countries gross domestic product grew at an average rate of 5 percent in the 1960s and 1970s and agricultural production at an average rate of 2.5 to 3 percent. Somewhat higher rates have been observed in middle-income countries and lower rates in the industrialized countries. The growth rates are predicted to slow in the low-income countries, but third world agriculture is likely to continue to grow at a 2 percent rate. Thus the theory and data surveyed in preceding chapters indicate that long-run global trends can be expected to continue.

Nevertheless, it remains difficult if not impossible to predict many of the key events likely to cause shorter-run deviations about the long-run global trend. Prediction becomes even more difficult as we move from analyzing highly aggregate entities, such as all developing countries, to individual countries. These difficulties were evident in the projections discussed in chapter 5.

Chapters 2 and 3 showed that various economic, political, and technological factors will determine the rate at which each country or region develops. Although it will remain difficult to predict how fast each country will develop, general economic principles can help us understand the conditions that will lead either to a successful growth path or to economic stagnation.

A basic premise of chapter 2 is that economic development is a process of capital accumulation, with capital broadly defined to include both the physical capital of firms and other kinds of human and social capital. This logic suggests that to predict growth we should look to the factors that either stimulate or constrain capital accumulation. In this way we should be able to differentiate countries that are likely to develop from those that are not.

Among the underlying factors that explain agricultural development are natural resource endowments and climate. Countries and regions with poor natural resource endowments are likely to be caught in the "poor but efficient" equilibrium described by Theodore W. Schultz: they will be poor because of the low productivity of their resources and technology even if they use their resources efficiently. Current examples are the semiarid tropical regions of the world, in south-central India, northern and sub-Saharan Africa, and parts of Latin America. It is difficult to see how those regions can realize significant economic growth with their present resources and technologies. Lacking a resource base with the capacity to produce savings for investment, they are unable to achieve higher productivity and higher incomes. Until agricultural researchers are able to devise plant varieties and animal breeds better suited to the semiarid environment, those regions are unlikely to be able to escape from their present circumstances. Unfortunately, few promising innovations are on the horizon.

Recent history provides examples of regions where the resource base was sufficiently rich, a more productive technology was made available, and significant development occurred. The Punjab of north India, parts of Indonesia and the Philippines, Thailand, and the newly industrialized countries (NICs) such as Taiwan and Korea are examples in Asia.[1] Significant success has been achieved in various South American countries as well. Some of this agricultural growth can be attributed to the plant breeding accomplishments of the international agricultural research centers, such as the International Maize and Wheat Improvement Center in Mexico and the International Rice Research Center in the Philippines. These successes also reflect local conditions favorable to the new agricultural technologies and an economic environment that encouraged investments in physical and human capital.

The political system and the government's economic policies are other major factors affecting capital accumulation in developing countries. Many countries with relatively rich resource endowments have not experienced economic development. The cause of the low growth rates in such cases is often political instability or economic policies that thwart incentives for capital accumulation. As noted in chapter 5, many policies either are designed to tax agriculture or have that effect. Such "taxes" can be imposed directly on producers or indirectly through government marketing boards, export taxes, or exchange rate policies. In addition, many governments in attempting to control input markets distort the innovation process. The net effect of such policies is to shift resources away from the most efficient use and to discourage capital investment in agriculture.[2]

Sub-Saharan Africa offers numerous examples of such policies and their consequences. The region has experienced great economic difficulties during the past decade, with per capita food production and real incomes falling in some countries. There the performance of agriculture is a key variable in economic performance, since agriculture accounts for 30 to 60 percent of aggregate income and for the majority of labor employment. Governments in sub-Saharan Africa have a history of taxing agriculture and intervening in production in ways that have disrupted agricultural production and created disincentives to invest and produce. The intervention in agriculture is more extreme than in other parts of the developing world, such as Asia and South America.[3] The political instability that has been a characteristic of many of these countries has created an uncertain economic environment not conducive to capital investment. Thus the evidence suggests that both government policies and political instability have aggravated the difficult problems caused by rapidly growing populations and poor resource bases in sub-Saharan African countries. There is little reason to believe that these patterns will not persist.

China is a major source of uncertainty in forecasting world agricultural development in the coming decades. Despite its political and economic policies of the 1960s and 1970s, which disrupted technological innovation in agriculture, a substantial growth rate in output has been achieved. The late 1970s and early 1980s have seen a move away from collectivization of agricultural production toward private enterprise and the use of economic incentives to increase productivity. Consequently, remarkable increases in agricultural output have been achieved during the past five years. China appears to have significant potential for future growth in production as well as in demand. It is difficult to predict whether the new policy regime will remain in place or whether the resulting productivity and income growth will be translated into higher import demand. Studies by the U.S. Department of Agriculture and the World Bank predict large growth in Chinese demand for food imports, but other studies suggest a much lower growth in imports. All these predictions are conditional on Chinese policy decisions, which are difficult to predict.[4]

What does seem fairly certain is that East Asia and the middle-income countries of Latin America are particularly well positioned to take advantage of new technology and new market opportunities.

With their well-developed transport and communications infrastructure, their large and growing stock of human capital, and their increasing democratization and political stability, they are also well positioned to take advantage of coming technological innovations, such as applications of biotechnology. This seems to be particularly true of East Asia, where most arable land is already under cultivation and growth in yields must come from land-saving innovations. East Asian countries have responded rapidly to the opportunities presented by the seed-fertilizer technology of the green revolution, and they seem equally prepared to adapt forthcoming biogenetic innovations to their local conditions.

In contrast to East Asia, many poor countries, such as those in sub-Saharan Africa, will find it difficult to take advantage of changes in world market conditions and biotechnological innovations. Those countries do not have the technological capability to adapt the new technology to their conditions readily, nor do they have the economic capacity to bring the fruits of rapid technological change to world markets.

These observations support the conclusion that the long-run trends in world agricultural development evident in the past two decades are likely to continue. Those countries that have risen from low- to middle-income ranks are likely to see continued improvements in real per capita incomes and continued growth in agricultural productivity and should thus continue to close the gap between themselves and the high-income countries. But the poorer countries will probably continue to lag far behind, and some seem destined to experience deterioration in real per capita incomes and in agricultural productivity.

The Relevance of the Asian Model

Many analysts of world agricultural trade point to certain rapidly growing Asian countries—such as Korea and Taiwan—as evidence that economic growth in the other developing countries must lead to growth in their demand for food imports. Can the rest of the developing world be expected to follow this Asian model?

The same economic principles that apply to the successful development of the newly industrialized countries also apply to the lower-income countries in South Asia, sub-Saharan Africa, and Latin America. There are important differences, however, between the NICs, such as Singapore, Taiwan, and Korea, and many of the poorer developing countries. First, the NICs are all quite small and densely populated, and their transportation costs are consequently low. In addition, they benefit from ready access to major ocean shipping lanes. In contrast, many African countries are large and sparsely populated. Costly investments in infrastructure are required to link agricultural producers with domestic and international markets. Many African countries are landlocked or are less well located than the NICs for international trade.

A second important difference between the NICs and the poorer developing countries, as documented in chapter 4, lies in their investments in social overhead capital. The gap between the NICs and the poorer developing countries is substantial in the investments in institutions and human capital needed to achieve rapid agricultural development.

Other social and political factors certainly must come into consideration as well. Unlike the culturally homogeneous Asian NICs, many poor developing countries suffer from social and political divisiveness caused by heterogeneous populations. In some African countries, for example, national boundaries were drawn by colonial powers with little regard for religious, tribal, or cultural patterns.

These considerations all point to economic, social, and political constraints on the development of many poorer third world countries that were not faced by the NICs. These constraints are likely to cause the larger, less geographically favored, more culturally diverse countries to continue to lag behind the growth of smaller, geographically favored, culturally homogeneous countries. If the disadvantaged countries do manage to achieve higher per capita incomes, we can expect to see the same changes in patterns of production and consumption that we have seen in the NICs. Relatively few countries, however, can be expected to undergo the kind of rapid change that was possible in the NICs. Thus the rapid growth in demand for food and feed grain imports that occurred in the NICs seems unlikely to be replicated by the rest of the developing world.

Technical Assistance and Foreign Competition

The United States provides technical assistance to other countries' agricultures directly through the U.S. Agency for International Development and indirectly through the activities of land-grant universities. Part of this assistance takes the form of transfer and development of production technology, often for major U.S. export crops, such as wheat, corn, and soybeans.

Two conflicting views are held on the role of technical assistance to less-developed countries. Those in favor of such assistance argue that it is morally good to help other countries feed themselves and believe that foreign assistance is in the economic and political self-interest of the United States. Economists argue that the United States can increase the demand for its export crops by stimulating income growth in importing countries.[5] U.S. agricultural interests, however, have argued that technical assistance, such as the development of high-yielding varieties of soybeans in Brazil, directly increases the competition faced by U.S. producers in world markets. In addressing this debate, it is important to note that two different questions are being raised. The question raised by farmers' interest groups is whether U.S. farmers gain or lose from technical assistance. The question raised by those in favor of technical assistance is whether the recipient country and the United States gain or lose from technical assistance.

The growth model of chapter 3 can be used to investigate these issues. Technical assistance to a developing country shifts out its production possibilities curve for the agricultural commodity but not for manufacturing. If the country is initially a net food importer, there are two effects: at given product prices, there is an increase in food production relative to production of manufactured goods; and the increased income from higher agricultural productivity enables the country to consume more of all types of goods. The net effect of these changes on the country's agricultural food imports depends on the relative increases of demand and production. The argument in favor of technical assistance is based on the premise that the United States tends to export products with relatively high income demand elasticities, so that demand for U.S. exports grows faster than production and imports increase. This is most likely to happen when the benefits of the technical assistance are equitably distributed throughout the society, especially to poorer households, which spend a large percentage of their incomes on food.

Even if technical assistance increases demand for imports, the increased demand need not be satisfied by U.S. products. All exporters of the products demanded can compete for the expanded market. The United States cannot prevent other countries from trying to benefit from demand increases stimulated by U.S. assistance.

Although the growth of demand for imports is a possible consequence of technical assistance, it is not the only possible outcome. Indeed, technical assistance for production of a single crop may not lead to a significant economy-wide increase in per capita income. This is especially likely to be true in countries where landownership is highly skewed or where the new technology created by the technical aid is regionally limited, so that the growth in income is realized by a small proportion of the population. In such cases crop production might easily grow faster than demand, so that the country would import less or even shift from being a net importer to being a net exporter.

There appear to be examples of both these possibilities. In Korea, where landownership is not highly concentrated and income growth has been widely distributed throughout the population, technological change led to income growth and thus to a much higher rate of growth in the demand for feed grains than in their domestic supply. In India, which was an importer of wheat and rice in the early 1960s, modern wheat and rice varieties were introduced in the mid-1960s, and stocks of wheat and rice increased. By the late 1970s India could even export wheat and rice in some years. By the mid-1980s it held large wheat stocks.[6] While production grew rapidly in the Punjab region of northern India, many parts of India did not experience significant income growth, and national demand failed to keep pace with production.

Another important factor in analyzing the effects of technical assistance is the specificity of the assistance. Helping a country to improve its transportation and communications infrastructure might contribute to overall economic growth and hence to import demand, whereas development of production methods for a specific crop might lead to a rapid growth of production without a corresponding growth of demand.

The conclusion, therefore, is that both arguments may be valid in specific circumstances. It would be wrong to argue categorically that either view holds in all cases. Moreover, even where technical assistance does increase another country's ability to compete with U.S. producers, it may be in the larger political interest of the United States to provide such assistance.

The effects of U.S. assistance on the growth of foreign competition may be very small. The transfer of technology to developing countries is largely beyond the control of the United States and will go on regardless of U.S. policy. It would be arrogant for the United States to believe that its technical assistance alone will determine the rate of production growth abroad; many other countries provide such assistance.

Equilibrium in U.S. Agriculture

D. Gale Johnson has argued that the U.S. agricultural sector was approaching an equilibrium in the early 1970s in the sense that real incomes in the farm and nonfarm sectors of the economy had been equalized. The factor market disequilibrium that characterizes the early stages of agricultural development had been eliminated, and a transfer of resources out of the sector was no longer needed.[7] In view of the continuing integration of U.S. agriculture into international markets and the changes that it necessitates, can we still conclude that U.S. agriculture has achieved this resource market equilibrium?

The theory and data presented in this study indicate that the worldwide movement of resources out of agriculture will continue because of continued growth in agricultural productivity. The increasing specialization in production suggested by this global scenario will affect the United States as well as other countries. The growth model discussed in chapter 3 shows that the decline in real incomes caused by lower prices can be offset by technological change. Because of technological change fewer resources, particularly land and labor, will be required to produce a growing output.

This scenario for the future implies that U.S. agriculture faces a kind of disequilibrium different from the disequilibrium it faced in the early part of the twentieth century. That disequilibrium was due to the economic forces associated with a growing closed economy. The movement of resources from the farm to the nonfarm sector was necessary to achieve the equilibrium condition in factor markets wherein equally productive resources (for example, labor of a particular skill level) are paid the same wage.

The internationalization of U.S. agriculture makes it increasingly subject to the forces of the international economy. The opening of the U.S. agricultural sector to trade also means that the state of equilibrium or disequilibrium in U.S. agriculture is determined to a significant degree by world market forces. This fact is illustrated by the events of the 1970s and 1980s. Farm and nonfarm incomes were roughly equal in the early 1970s, but farm incomes surpassed nonfarm incomes in the mid-1970s because of the rapid growth in demand for U.S. exports. With the fall in U.S. exports in the early 1980s, farm income fell to the levels of the 1960s.[8] This series of events illustrates both the ineffectiveness of existing price policies in setting farm incomes and the extent to which general world economic conditions and world commodity market conditions affect U.S. farm income.

The exodus of labor from U.S. agriculture in the early part of the twentieth century will not be repeated in the latter part, simply because many fewer workers are employed in agriculture. This does not mean, however, that the numbers of farm operations cannot continue to decline. Indeed, further significant declines seem likely in view of continued growth in agricultural productivity in excess of growth in demand. Some 880,000 farms produced about 80 percent of all agricultural output in the United States in 1970. The number of farms required to produce 80 percent of output declined to 530,000 by 1985, a reduction of 40 percent in fifteen years. If this trend were to continue to the year 2000, about 300,000 farms would produce 80 percent of output. At that rate about 15,000 farms per year (from the group of farms that produce 80 percent of output) would have to leave the industry.

Addressing the question of equilibrium for U.S. agriculture is another way of posing the fundamental question of this study: What major trends are likely to affect U.S. agriculture in the near and longer terms? The growth model discussed in chapter 3 and the data presented in chapters 4 and 5 suggest that, to maintain the income equilibrium recognized by Johnson, the forces of world agricultural development abroad and technological change at home will require continuing change in U.S. agriculture. The changes dictated by technology and market conditions may well mean fewer family farms in U.S. agriculture. U.S. policy can try to resist this change, but only at the expense of incurring increasingly higher costs in the form of subsidies to keep marginal producers in operation.

U.S. Agricultural Policy

Modern U.S. agricultural policy was shaped in the years of the Great Depression. At that time the problems of agriculture were perceived to be the inherent instability of commodity markets, which caused instability in farm incomes, and a secular income problem due to the persistence of excess resources, especially labor, in agriculture. Beginning with the Agricultural Adjustment Act of 1933, major commodity programs were introduced in response to the crushing effects of the depression. The enactment of this law marked the beginning of modern American agricultural policy. Corn, cotton, milk, peanuts, rice, tobacco, and wheat were the principal commodities for agricultural policy. Programs were devised to support prices either through voluntary or mandatory removal of acreage from production or through removal of surplus product from markets.[9]

The programs devised in the 1930s remain essentially intact, although they have undergone various modifications. Four means of intervention are in use: price supports operated by government purchases of commodities (through the provision of nonrecourse loans at the "loan rate," that is, the support price); acreage and production controls; payments to farmers based on the difference between market prices and target prices set by government policy; and trade intervention, especially import controls and, sporadically, export subsidies.

In the 1950s the federal government's direct intervention in major commodity markets led to the accumulation of large stocks.[10] Although it was not clear that these policies raised or stabilized farm incomes as intended, they did keep prices above the market-clearing level and led to substantial increases in production. The resulting commodity stock buildups and their associated storage and management costs led to attempts by the U.S. government to dispose of the stocks abroad through export subsidies and the Food for Peace program (Public Law 480), enacted in 1954. The federal government also attempted to modify its approach to market intervention with the Agricultural Act of 1954 by moving to more flexible price supports, although most of the changes in the 1954 act were not implemented. Unfortunately, acreage controls rather than output quotas were maintained, which in combination with high price supports led to still further excess production. Acreage control remains part of U.S. policy despite its obvious inefficiencies.

Since the 1960s U.S. agricultural policy has gradually moved toward separation of market intervention and income support. The Food and Agricultural Act of 1965 introduced policy modifications that have remained in place. Price supports were allowed to follow shifts in market conditions more closely, and incomes were supported through direct payments to farmers in connection with acreage control. Target prices and deficiency payments were introduced as a means of transferring income without intervening directly in commodity markets. Not surprisingly, economists and legislators have had continuing difficulty in devising a scheme to determine target prices. The 1977 food bill reportedly based target prices on the cost of production, a difficult task since major components of the cost of production, notably land rents, themselves depend on product prices. Difficulties associated with the setting of target prices continued to plague the writing of the 1981 and 1985 farm bills.[11]

The 1981 farm bill appears to have been written partly in response to the fears of the late 1970s that a world food crisis was at hand. Despite informed opinion and much evidence to the contrary, the bill set high target and support prices, which served to maintain world prices for traded commodities, notably wheat, above market-clearing prices.[12] The subsequent accumulation of stocks of cereals was a motive for the the payment-in-kind (PIK) program of 1983, which was intended to reduce production by inducing farmers to leave land idle in exchange for payments made with commodities held by the government. Combined with a higher participation rate than expected, a below average corn crop due to bad weather, and exchange rate and macroeconomic disturbances, these policies resulted in massive payments to farmers and continued declines in U.S. exports.

The 1985 farm bill debate, in a dramatic reversal of the debate over the 1981 bill, centered on the problems of chronic overproduction rather than on a world food crisis. Because of unrealistically high support prices set by the 1981 farm bill, the cost of farm programs increased from about $3 billion in the early 1980s to nearly $8 billion in 1985 and is expected to continue to increase.[13] U.S. exports of cereals declined significantly during the early 1980s, and the decline contributed to the difficulties of U.S. agriculture brought on by a general economic recession, historically high interest rates, and an unfavorable exchange rate. In addition, farmers bore the brunt of global politics as President Jimmy Carter's 1980 grain embargo took effect. Many farm groups and economists argued that these policies contributed to the loss of grain markets by the U.S. industry, although that proposition remains controversial and has been disputed by a major study.[14]

Other important components of U.S. agricultural policy during the past several decades have been the continuing support of public sector research and development and foreign aid to developing countries for general economic development as well as agricultural development. As U.S. export market shares declined in the early 1980s, foreign agricultural assistance for agricultural research became controversial. As noted earlier in this chapter, the effects of foreign technical assistance on U.S. agriculture may be positive or negative, depending on whether the assistance stimulates income growth in the recipient country.

The 1985 farm bill largely preserved the spirit of the farm legislation of the past twenty years but made some changes in it. Target prices remained high, and a phased-in lowering of loan rates was built into the law. It has been argued that the lowering of loan rates is a move toward greater "market orientation"; yet the cost of direct payments to farmers in 1986 was reportedly over $26 billion, up from $2.2 billion in 1980. Thus while the policy rhetoric and some aspects of policy have moved toward a greater market orientation, it remains to be seen whether the overall thrust of agricultural policy, as actually implemented, will do so.

While not fundamentally different from previous farm legislation, the 1985 farm bill differed from its predecessors of the 1960s and 1970s in its conservation provisions. It created the Conservation Reserve Program, whose goal was to remove from production land that was judged to be highly erodable, estimated to be as much as 10 percent of total cropland. Moreover, the 1985 legislation made compliance with land conservation provisions of the bill a requirement for continued participation in commodity programs. In 1987 some 6 percent of farmland had been put into the conservation reserve, most of it in the western states.

The 1985 farm bill also reintroduced export subsidies, which it labeled the "export enhancement program." In 1987 and 1988 federal authorities used this program to eliminate a large share of grain stocks they had acquired in the early 1980s.

What Is Wrong with U.S. Policy. U.S. agricultural policy was formulated in the years of the Great Depression, when the "farm problem" was associated with the chronic excess supply of resources—especially human resources—in agriculture and with incomes below those outside farming. Agricultural markets were viewed as less stable than other markets, because of the inelasticity of demand and weather shocks on the supply side, leading to highly unstable farm incomes. The solution to these problems was thought to be government intervention in agricultural markets to keep prices at "fair" levels, which in practice came to mean above market equilibrium, and to stabilize markets by buying when prices were low and selling when they were high.[15]

The analysis in chapter 3 implies that the fundamental source of disequilibrium in U.S. agriculture in the early twentieth century, as in all developing agricultures, was the presence of excess resources, especially human labor. Thus the appropriate policy response by the government would have been to facilitate the transfer of those resources out of the agricultural sector. This kind of policy could have been implemented in various ways—for example, by ensuring that rural education provided the skills demanded in the nonagricultural sector.

The appropriate policy response to excess labor in agriculture is not to support prices above market-clearing levels. In the short run a price support policy raises farm income and thus transmits the wrong price signals to farmers deciding whether to stay in agriculture or move to nonagricultural employment. In the longer run price and income support programs further distort decision making as the value of the commodity programs is capitalized into farm assets. Farmers who own assets when the policy is invoked gain through the increased value of their assets and do not perceive the correct economic signal about the long-run economic viability of their farms. Farmers

87

who subsequently want to buy into farming must pay the capitalized value of the farm programs and thus do not benefit from the economic transfers brought about by the price or income support programs. Instead, they need larger amounts of financial capital to enter into the business of farming. Once they do enter, ironically, their economic survival depends on the existence of the support programs. Having had to pay the capitalized value of the programs to enter, they need the high program prices and income transfers to break even. At lower market equilibrium prices or without income support, farmers who paid the high land prices caused by these policies would be insolvent.

In a closed economy a policy that keeps prices above market equilibrium for a substantial period inevitably encourages production beyond market-clearing levels. Hence the chronic problem of "surplus" production in the United States and other countries (notably those of the EC) using this kind of policy. The continuing production of surplus product puts downward pressure on prices to levels far below the "fair" level as defined by policy. Consequently, to maintain prices at their support levels, the government must continually remove surplus commodities from the market. Stock accumulation has thus been one of the legacies of the U.S. commodity programs. More recently both the EC and the United States have resorted to export subsidies to reduce stocks thus acquired.

Price support programs also do little to solve the farm problem because farmers' incomes are increasingly determined by nonfarm income. The percentage of farm family income earned by farming dropped from 55 percent in 1960 to less than 40 percent in the early 1980s and continues to decline.[16]

Nor is it clear that commodity price policies stabilize farm incomes. Since a growing percentage of incomes of farm people is earned from the nonfarm sector, their incomes depend increasingly on the state of the general economy. In addition, not all risks in agriculture are price risks; production risk is important and is not affected by price support programs. The integration of U.S. agriculture into world markets means that demand and supply shocks from around the world are transmitted, to varying degrees, to the U.S. farm sector. Commodity programs can also introduce an element of uncertainty into commodity markets. Indeed, the continual revision of government farm policies is testament to the extent of "policy risk" in agriculture.

U.S. agricultural policy distorts production decisions and prevents U.S. agriculture from taking advantage of its remarkable natural endowments of soil and climate. The United States possesses a large share of the world's fertile arable land in the temperate climate zone and thus has a comparative advantage in production of major traded commodities, especially cereals.[17] U.S. policy also distorts production decisions abroad because the United States supplies such a large part of the world trade in cereals. This was demonstrated by the experience of the early 1980s, when the high U.S. loan rate set the world price for wheat. That policy encouraged production to take place in marginal areas around the world that would not be in production at lower world market equilibrium prices. Thus U.S. policy not only distorts U.S. production away from its comparative advantage but contributes to the distortion of production decisions throughout the world. Consequently, the U.S. share in commodity trade declines, and the United States fails to exploit its comparative advantage.

The U.S. policy of subsidizing exports in the mid-1980s constituted a curious reversal of the policy of the early 1980s. Although this policy change was described as an attempt to move U.S. agriculture toward greater market orientation, it remains to be seen whether the subsidies will actually accomplish that goal, since the U.S. policy will continue to restrict acreage and transfer large amounts of income to farmers through diversion payments. As long as the United States continues to restrict its production significantly, international markets will be distorted, and production patterns around the world will not follow comparative advantage.

Under a free market policy, not only would the price support mechanism be abandoned, allowing world market prices to decline to equilibrium, but production controls would be eliminated. In the short run U.S. farmers would have to absorb the decapitalization of the value of the support policy from their assets. But at the same time inefficient producers in other parts of the world would leave the industry. In the longer run the United States would regain its market share in trade while producing efficiently.

It has been argued that a price support policy or an output control policy is desirable because the United States possesses market power in the international commodity markets.[18] But the events of the early 1980s raise serious questions about the wisdom of such a policy. The recent experience with wheat shows that U.S. monopoly power is indeed limited by the large amount of land around the world that can be converted to wheat cultivation when the price is high. Moreover, with agricultural development continuing throughout the world, a growing global productive capacity can replace U.S. agricultural production in world markets if the United States attempts to exploit its monopoly power. Thus it would be very shortsighted for the United States to believe that it could exploit such market power even in the short run.

Needed Changes in U.S. Policy. Various changes in U.S. agricultural policy have been suggested in the debates over farm legislation. The debate over the 1985 farm bill was no exception.[19] This section examines policy change in the context of the international economic environment in which U.S. agriculture is now operating.

U.S. policy is formulated in four-year farm bills. In practice farm policy has changed more frequently than at four-year intervals because of congressional modifications of the existing law or changes in programs that are at the discretion of the secretary of agriculture. Farm policy can be inflexible; the 1981 farm bill, for example, set support prices too high in light of changes that subsequently took place in the national and international economies. Policy has also been ,subject to whimsical changes, such as the decision to implement the 1983 PIK program. To enable farm managers to make rational investment and marketing decisions, agricultural policy needs to be both stable and flexible. That is, policy rules need to be established for an announced period and to be designed so as not to come into conflict with changes in market conditions that cannot be anticipated by policy makers.

Despite the claims that present policy is moving in the direction of greater market orientation, these policies continue to constitute a major obstacle to achieving a more technologically dynamic and price-responsive sector. The target price and deficiency payment scheme, while accomplishing to a certain degree a "decoupling" of production decisions and income support, continues to be a very inflexible system that discourages farmers from reallocating their resources according to price signals. In particular, participation in the present system depends on the farmer's established acreage "base" in the program crop. Many farmers thus become more concerned with establishing and maintaining their base than with the economically efficient use of their land and other resources. This system clearly provides a strong disincentive for farmers to allocate their land away from the program crops, even when market prices and technological changes are signaling that a different use of the land would be economically efficient. Thus it is far from clear that the reliance on the target price system will in fact reflect any greater degree of market orientation than the earlier reliance on price supports. Indeed, it appears possible that the target price system could result in greater distortions in resource allocation.

Similar potential problems exist with the new Conservation Reserve Program. Despite its laudable conservation objectives, it remains to be seen whether the participation rules established by the U.S. Department of Agriculture actually accomplish conservation goals. Will, for example, the vast acreage being put into the program be land that is "highly erodable," or will it simply be any land with expected returns below those promised by the program? Moreover, many farmers in western states are questioning the long-term effects of the program because of unanticipated effects on the farm economy, on the one hand, and on other environmental problems such as weed control, on the other hand. And the inflexibility of the program—land must be committed to it for ten years—again seems likely to work against the ability of the U.S. farm sector to respond to changes in world market conditions. Thus, like other U.S. programs, the Conservation Reserve Program appears to move U.S. agriculture away from the path of productive efficiency indicated by principles of comparative advantage.

Given the need for prices to be determined in the world commodity markets, the United States needs to move away from its existing policies by phasing out the system of loan rates and target prices. It can be argued that an equitable policy would include some form of lump-sum transfer to farmers to compensate them for the decapitalization of assets that would be caused by this policy change. If American taxpayers decide that income transfers to farm families are desirable, those transfers should be decoupled from farmers' decisions about production and the allocation of resources. Income transfers unrelated to production decisions will encourage more farmers to stay in agriculture, but they will not distort the decisions of those who are in the industry. This kind of policy will achieve income transfers to farmers at a lower cost to society than the existing system.

U.S. agriculture will be increasingly affected by the policies of other countries through its growing integration in world agricultural markets. This will be especially true of the policies of major trading blocks such as the EC, the Soviet Union and Eastern Europe, China, Canada, Brazil, and India. Given the magnitude of those countries' production and consumption and their present or possible future involvement in international commodity markets, a major change in policy in any one of them can have significant effects on the United States. In contrast, many developing countries are relatively small, and their policy changes are unlikely to have major international effects. These facts again point to the need for a flexible U.S. policy that relies on world market prices. It is impossible for policy makers to predict the kinds of events that lead to changes in world markets.

Hence price support policies are bound to be at odds with world market conditions, distorting production and marketing decisions and ultimately working to the competitive disadvantage of U.S. agriculture.

Summary

The data and projections in the preceding chapters provide what may be reasonably accurate predictions of the long-run trends in population and technological change. Even if these predictions enabled us to make accurate long-run predictions of demand and supply, substantial short-run variations in production and demand are likely around the long-run trend. Those variations will be due to weather as well as to political and economic change. Predicting changes in national policies is probably even more difficult than predicting the weather. It seems fair to say that the coming decades will see continuing instability in international markets induced by vagaries in the natural and political climates around the world.[20] Given the importance of international trade to the future of U.S. agriculture, general economic and trade policies will become increasingly important to agriculture.

Thus instead of remaining traditionally oriented to commodities, U.S. policy needs to be concerned with the role of U.S. agriculture in the national and international economies. Because of the increasing importance of that role, agricultural policy should be addressing the following kinds of questions:

• How do national monetary and fiscal policies affect agriculture?
• Do existing trade policies result in unfair competition by foreign producers? Do other countries subsidize their agricultures more than the United States? If so, what policies should the United States pursue?
• Are U.S. policies on development assistance designed to encourage the economic growth in existing and potential trading partners that would generate a growth in demand for U.S. agricultural products?
• Do domestic policy objectives, such as income transfer and conservation, conflict with trade policy? Can we design policies so as to mitigate such conflicts?[21]

Notes

1. See John W. Mellor, *The New Economics of Growth* (Ithaca, N.Y.: Cornell University Press, 1976); and Richard Critchfield, *Villages* (New York: Anchor Press, 1983).

2. See Theodore W. Schultz, ed., *Distortions of Agricultural Incentives* (Bloomington: Indiana University Press, 1978).

3. See S. Singh, *Sub-Saharan Africa: Synthesis and Trade Prospects*, World Bank Working Paper no. 608, 1983; Peter J. Malton and Dunstan S. Spencer, "Increasing Food Production in Sub-Saharan Africa: Environmental Problems and Inadequate Technological Solutions," *American Journal of Agricultural Economics*, vol. 66 (1984), pp. 671–76; and Arthur J. Dommen, "Increasing Food Production in Sub-Saharan Africa: Comment," *American Journal of Agricultural Economics*, vol. 68 (1986), pp. 998–99.

4. U.S. Department of Agriculture, Economic Research Service, *China Situation and Outlook Report*, July 1986; World Bank, *China: Long-Term Development Issues and Options* (Baltimore: Johns Hopkins University Press, 1985); and Colin Carter and Fu-Ning Zhong, "China's Past and Future Role in Grain Trade," Department of Agricultural Economics, University of California, Davis, March 1987.

5. See John W. Mellor, *The Economics of Agricultural Development* (Ithaca, N.Y.: Cornell University Press, 1966).

6. U.S. Department of Agriculture, Economic Research Service, *South Asia Outlook and Situation Report*, August 1985.

7. D. Gale Johnson, *Farm Commodity Programs: An Opportunity for Change* (Washington, D.C.: American Enterprise Institute, 1973).

8. U.S. Department of Agriculture, *Economic Indicators of the Farm Sector: National Financial Summary, 1985*, National Economics Division, Economic Research Service.

9. Wayne D. Rasmussen and Gladys L. Baker, "Programs for Agriculture, 1933–1965," in Vernon W. Ruttan, Arley D. Waldo, and James P. Houck, eds., *Agricultural Policy in an Affluent Society* (New York: W. W. Norton & Co., 1969).

10. Willard W. Cochrane and Mary E. Ryan, *American Farm Policy, 1948–73* (Minneapolis: University of Minnesota Press, 1976).

11. See D. Gale Johnson, "Agricultural Policy Alternatives for the 1980s," in D. Gale Johnson, ed., *Food and Agricultural Policy for the 1980s* (Washington, D.C.: American Enterprise Institute, 1981).

12. D. Gale Johnson, "World Commodity Situation and Outlook," in Bruce L. Gardner, ed., *U.S. Agricultural Policy: The 1985 Farm Legislation* (Washington, D.C.: American Enterprise Institute, 1985).

13. U.S. Department of Agriculture, *Economic Indicators of the Farm Sector: National Financial Summary, 1985*, National Economics Division, Economic Research Service.

14. U.S. Department of Agriculture, Economic Research Service, *Embargoes, Surplus Disposal, and U.S. Agriculture*, Agricultural Economics Report no. 564, December 1986.

15. The concept of "parity" is often mentioned in the discussion of fair prices for agricultural products. Parity originally referred to prices comparable in real terms to the prices of the 1910–1914 period.

16. Johnson, "World Commodity Situation and Outlook."

17. For a further discussion of the comparative advantage of the United States in agriculture, see Thomas Vollrath, "Dynamics of Comparative Advan-

tage," U.S. Department of Agriculture, Economic Research Service, Foreign Agricultural Economics Report no. 214, August 1985.

18. See Andrew Schmitz, Alex McCalla, Donald Mitchell, and Colin Carter, *Grain Export Cartels* (Cambridge, Mass.: Ballinger, 1981).

19. Among the volumes of material generated by the 1985 farm bill, see Gardner, *U.S. Agricultural Policy*; Kenneth R. Farrell and Gordon C. Rausser, eds., *Alternative Agriculture and Food Policies and the 1985 Farm Bill* (Berkeley, Calif.: Giannini Foundation of Agricultural Economics, 1984); Harold O. Carter, ed., *The Impact of Farm Policy and Technological Change on U.S. and California Agriculture* (Davis: University of California Agricultural Issues Center, October 1986); and Council of Economic Advisers, *The Economic Report of the President, 1985*.

20. One country's policies can have counterintuitive effects on another country. For example, D. Gale Johnson has noted that attempts by one country to stabilize its prices are likely to have a destabilizing effect on world markets. See D. Gale Johnson, "World Agriculture, Commodity Policy, and Price Variability," *American Journal of Agricultural Economics*, vol. 57 (1975), pp. 823–38.

21. For example, pesticide restrictions in the United States motivated by the presence of pesticide residues on fruit may harm U.S. producers and cause the United States to import from other countries commodities that have been produced with the same pesticides. Can policies be designed to address such diverse issues as trade and environmental quality?

Index

A NOTE ON THE BOOK

This book was edited by Trudy Kaplan of the
publications staff of the American Enterprise Institute.
The figures were drawn by Hördur Karlsson,
and the index was prepared by Julia Petrakis.
The text was set in Palatino, a typeface designed by Hermann Zapf.
Coghill Book Typesetting Company, of Richmond, Virginia,
set the type, and Edwards Brothers Incorporated,
of Ann Arbor, Michigan, printed and bound the book,
using permanent, acid-free paper.